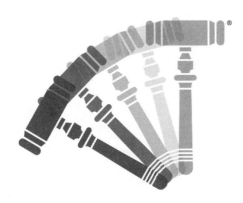

Casenote™ *Legal Briefs*

PROFESSIONAL RESPONSIBILITY

Keyed to Courses Using

Gillers's
Regulation of Lawyers

Eighth Edition

Wolters Kluwer
Law & Business

AUSTIN   BOSTON   CHICAGO   NEW YORK   THE NETHERLANDS

This publication is designed to provide accurate and authoritative information in regard to the subject matter covered. It is sold with the understanding that the publisher is not engaged in rendering legal, accounting, or other professional services. If legal advice or other expert assistance is required, the services of a competent professional person should be sought.

— From a Declaration of Principles adopted jointly by a Committee of the American Bar Association and a Committee of Publishers and Associates

To contact Customer Care, e-mail customer.care@aspenpublishers.com, call 1-800-234-1660, fax 1-800-901-9075, or mail correspondence to:

Aspen Publishers
Attn: Order Department
P.O. Box 990
Frederick, MD 21705

Printed in the United States of America.

1 2 3 4 5 6 7 8 9 0

ISBN 978-0-7355-7843-2

About Wolters Kluwer Law & Business

Wolters Kluwer Law & Business is a leading provider of research information and workflow solutions in key specialty areas. The strengths of the individual brands of Aspen Publishers, CCH, Kluwer Law International and Loislaw are aligned within Wolters Kluwer Law & Business to provide comprehensive, in-depth solutions and expert-authored content for the legal, professional and education markets.

CCH was founded in 1913 and has served more than four generations of business professionals and their clients. The CCH products in the Wolters Kluwer Law & Business group are highly regarded electronic and print resources for legal, securities, antitrust and trade regulation, government contracting, banking, pension, payroll, employment and labor, and health-care reimbursement and compliance professionals.

Aspen Publishers is a leading information provider for attorneys, business professionals and law students. Written by preeminent authorities, Aspen products offer analytical and practical information in a range of specialty practice areas from securities law and intellectual property to mergers and acquisitions and pension/benefits. Aspen's trusted legal education resources provide professors and students with high-quality, up-to-date and effective resources for successful instruction and study in all areas of the law.

Kluwer Law International supplies the global business community with comprehensive English-language international legal information. Legal practitioners, corporate counsel and business executives around the world rely on the Kluwer Law International journals, loose-leafs, books and electronic products for authoritative information in many areas of international legal practice.

Loislaw is a premier provider of digitized legal content to small law firm practitioners of various specializations. Loislaw provides attorneys with the ability to quickly and efficiently find the necessary legal information they need, when and where they need it, by facilitating access to primary law as well as state-specific law, records, forms and treatises.

Wolters Kluwer Law & Business, a unit of Wolters Kluwer, is headquartered in New York and Riverwoods, Illinois. Wolters Kluwer is a leading multinational publisher and information services company.

Format for the Casenote Legal Brief

Nature of Case: This section identifies the form of action (e.g., breach of contract, negligence, battery), the type of proceeding (e.g., demurrer, appeal from trial court's jury instructions) or the relief sought (e.g., damages, injunction, criminal sanctions).

Fact Summary: This is included to refresh your memory and can be used as a quick reminder of the facts.

Rule of Law: Summarizes the general principle of law that the case illustrates. It may be used for instant recall of the court's holding and for classroom discussion or home review.

Facts: This section contains all relevant facts of the case, including the contentions of the parties and the lower court holdings. It is written in a logical order to give the student a clear understanding of the case. The plaintiff and defendant are identified by their proper names throughout and are always labeled with a (P) or (D).

Party ID: Quick identification of the relationship between the parties.

Concurrence/Dissent: All concurrences and dissents are briefed whenever they are included by the casebook editor.

Analysis: This last paragraph gives you a broad understanding of where the case "fits in" with other cases in the section of the book and with the entire course. It is a hornbook-style discussion indicating whether the case is a majority or minority opinion and comparing the principal case with other cases in the casebook. It may also provide analysis from restatements, uniform codes, and law review articles. The analysis will prove to be invaluable to classroom discussion.

Palsgraf v. Long Island R.R. Co.

Injured bystander (P) v. Railroad company (D)

N.Y. Ct. App., 248 N.Y. 339, 162 N.E. 99 (1928).

NATURE OF CASE: Appeal from judgment affirming verdict for plaintiff seeking damages for personal injury.

FACT SUMMARY: Helen Palsgraf (P) was injured on R.R.'s (D) train platform when R.R.'s (D) guard helped a passenger aboard a moving train, causing his package to fall on the tracks. The package contained fireworks which exploded, creating a shock that tipped a scale onto Palsgraf (P).

🏛 RULE OF LAW
The risk reasonably to be perceived defines the duty to be obeyed.

FACTS: Helen Palsgraf (P) purchased a ticket to Rockaway Beach from R.R. (D) and was waiting on the train platform. As she waited, two men ran to catch a train that was pulling out from the platform. The first man jumped aboard, but the second man, who appeared as if he might fall, was helped aboard by the guard on the train who had kept the door open so they could jump aboard. A guard on the platform also helped by pushing him onto the train. The man was carrying a package wrapped in newspaper. In the process, the man dropped his package, which fell on the tracks. The package contained fireworks and exploded. The shock of the explosion was apparently of great enough strength to tip over some scales at the other end of the platform, which fell on Palsgraf (P) and injured her. A jury awarded her damages, and R.R. (D) appealed.

ISSUE: Does the risk reasonably to be perceived define the duty to be obeyed?

HOLDING AND DECISION: (Cardozo, C.J.) Yes. The risk reasonably to be perceived defines the duty to be obeyed. If there is no foreseeable hazard to the injured party as the result of a seemingly innocent act, the act does not become a tort because it happened to be a wrong as to another. If the wrong was not willful, the plaintiff must show that the act as to her had such great and apparent possibilities of danger as to entitle her to protection. Negligence in the abstract is not enough upon which to base liability. Negligence is a relative concept, evolving out of the common law doctrine of trespass on the case. To establish liability, the defendant must owe a legal duty of reasonable care to the injured party. A cause of action in tort will lie where harm,

though unintended, could have been averted or avoided by observance of such a duty. The scope of the duty is limited by the range of danger that a reasonable person could foresee. In this case, there was nothing to suggest from the appearance of the parcel or otherwise that the parcel contained fireworks. The guard could not reasonably have had any warning of a threat to Palsgraf (P), and R.R. (D) therefore cannot be held liable. Judgment is reversed in favor of R.R. (D).

DISSENT: (Andrews, J.) The concept that there is no negligence unless R.R. (D) owes a legal duty to take care as to Palsgraf (P) herself is too narrow. Everyone owes to the world at large the duty of refraining from those acts that may unreasonably threaten the safety of others. If the guard's action was negligent as to those nearby, it was also negligent as to those outside what might be termed the "danger zone." For Palsgraf (P) to recover, R.R.'s (D) negligence must have been the proximate cause of her injury, a question of fact for the jury.

▶ ANALYSIS

The majority defined the limit of the defendant's liability in terms of the danger that a reasonable person in defendant's situation would have perceived. The dissent argued that the limitation should not be placed on liability, but rather on damages. Judge Andrews suggested that only injuries that would not have happened but for R.R.'s (D) negligence should be compensable. Both the majority and dissent recognized the policy-driven need to limit liability for negligent acts, seeking, in the words of Judge Andrews, to define a framework "that will be practical and in keeping with the general understanding of mankind." The Restatement (Second) of Torts has accepted Judge Cardozo's view.

Quicknotes

FORESEEABILITY A reasonable expectation that change is the probable result of certain acts or omissions.

NEGLIGENCE Conduct falling below the standard of care that a reasonable person would demonstrate under similar conditions.

PROXIMATE CAUSE The natural sequence of events without which an injury would not have been sustained.

Issue: The issue is a concise question that brings out the essence of the opinion as it relates to the section of the casebook in which the case appears. Both substantive and procedural issues are included if relevant to the decision.

Holding and Decision: This section offers a clear and in-depth discussion of the rule of the case and the court's rationale. It is written in easy-to-understand language and answers the issue presented by applying the law to the facts of the case. When relevant, it includes a thorough discussion of the exceptions to the case as listed by the court, any major cites to the other cases on point, and the names of the judges who wrote the decisions.

Quicknotes: Conveniently defines legal terms found in the case and summarizes the nature of any statutes, codes, or rules referred to in the text.

Note to Students

Aspen Publishers is proud to offer *Casenote Legal Briefs*—continuing thirty years of publishing America's best-selling legal briefs.

Casenote Legal Briefs are designed to help you save time when briefing assigned cases. Organized under convenient headings, they show you how to abstract the basic facts and holdings from the text of the actual opinions handed down by the courts. Used as part of a rigorous study regimen, they can help you spend more time analyzing and critiquing points of law than on copying bits and pieces of judicial opinions into your notebook or outline.

Casenote Legal Briefs should never be used as a substitute for assigned casebook readings. They work best when read as a follow-up to reviewing the underlying opinions themselves. Students who try to avoid reading and digesting the judicial opinions in their casebooks or online sources will end up shortchanging themselves in the long run. The ability to absorb, critique, and restate the dynamic and complex elements of case law decisions is crucial to your success in law school and beyond. It cannot be developed vicariously.

Casenote Legal Briefs represents but one of the many offerings in Aspen's Study Aid Timeline, which includes:

- *Casenote Legal Briefs*
- *Emanuel Law Outlines*
- *Examples & Explanations* Series
- *Introduction to Law* Series
- Emanuel *Law in a Flash* Flashcards
- Emanuel *CrunchTime* Series

Each of these series is designed to provide you with easy-to-understand explanations of complex points of law. Each volume offers guidance on the principles of legal analysis and, consulted regularly, will hone your ability to spot relevant issues. We have titles that will help you prepare for class, prepare for your exams, and enhance your general comprehension of the law along the way.

To find out more about Aspen Study Aid publications, visit us online at *http://lawschool.aspenpublishers.com* or email us at *legaledu@wolterskluwer.com*. We'll be happy to assist you.

Get this Casenote Legal Brief as an AspenLaw Studydesk eBook today!

By returning this form to Aspen Publishers, you will receive a complimentary eBook download of this Casenote Legal Brief in the AspenLaw Studydesk digital format.* Learn more about AspenLaw Studydesk today at *www.AspenLaw.com.*

Name	Phone ( )

Address		Apt. No.

City	State	ZIP Code

Law School	Year (check one) □ 1st □ 2nd □ 3rd

Cut out the UPC found on the lower left corner of the back cover of this book. Staple the UPC inside this box. Only the original UPC from the book cover will be accepted. (No photocopies or store stickers are allowed.)

Attach UPC inside this box.

Email (Print legibly or you may not get access!)

Title of this book (course subject)

ISBN of this book (10- or 13-digit number on the UPC)

Used with which casebook (provide author's name)

Mail the completed form to:

Aspen Publishers, Inc.
Legal Education Division
130 Turner Street, Bldg 3, 4th Floor
Waltham, MA 02453-8901

* Upon receipt of this completed form, you will be emailed a code for the digital download of this book in AspenLaw Studydesk format. The AspenLaw Studydesk application is available as a 60-day free trial at *www.AspenLaw.com.*

For a full list of print titles by Aspen Publishers, visit *lawschool.aspenpublishers.com.*
For a full list of digital eBook titles by Aspen Publishers, visit *www.AspenLaw.com.*

Make a photocopy of this form and your UPC for your records.

For detailed information on the use of the information you provide on this form, please see the PRIVACY POLICY at www.aspenpublishers.com.

A. Decide on a Format and Stick to It

Structure is essential to a good brief. It enables you to arrange systematically the related parts that are scattered throughout most cases, thus making manageable and understandable what might otherwise seem to be an endless and unfathomable sea of information. There are, of course, an unlimited number of formats that can be utilized. However, it is best to find one that suits your needs and stick to it. Consistency breeds both efficiency and the security that when called upon you will know where to look in your brief for the information you are asked to give.

Any format, as long as it presents the essential elements of a case in an organized fashion, can be used. Experience, however, has led *Casenotes* to develop and utilize the following format because of its logical flow and universal applicability.

NATURE OF CASE: This is a brief statement of the legal character and procedural status of the case (e.g., "Appeal of a burglary conviction").

There are many different alternatives open to a litigant dissatisfied with a court ruling. The key to determining which one has been used is to discover *who is asking this court for what.*

This first entry in the brief should be kept as *short as possible.* Use the court's terminology if you understand it. But since jurisdictions vary as to the titles of pleadings, the best entry is the one that addresses who wants what in this proceeding, not the one that sounds most like the court's language.

RULE OF LAW: A statement of the general principle of law that the case illustrates (e.g., "An acceptance that varies any term of the offer is considered a rejection and counteroffer").

Determining the rule of law of a case is a procedure similar to determining the issue of the case. Avoid being fooled by red herrings; there may be a few rules of law mentioned in the case excerpt, but usually only one is *the* rule with which the casebook editor is concerned. The techniques used to locate the issue, described below, may also be utilized to find the rule of law. Generally, your best guide is simply the chapter heading. It is a clue to the point the casebook editor seeks to make and should be kept in mind when reading every case in the respective section.

FACTS: A synopsis of only the essential facts of the case, i.e., those bearing upon or leading up to the issue.

The facts entry should be a short statement of the events and transactions that led one party to initiate legal proceedings against another in the first place. While some cases conveniently state the salient facts at the beginning of the decision, in other instances they will have to be culled from hiding places throughout the text, even from concurring and dissenting opinions. Some of the "facts" will often be in dispute and should be so noted. Conflicting evidence may be briefly pointed up. "Hard" facts must be included. Both must be *relevant* in order to be listed in the facts entry. It is impossible to tell what is relevant until the entire case is read, as the ultimate determination of the rights and liabilities of the parties may turn on something buried deep in the opinion.

Generally, the facts entry should not be longer than three to five *short* sentences.

It is often helpful to identify the role played by a party in a given context. For example, in a construction contract case the identification of a party as the "contractor" or "builder" alleviates the need to tell that that party was the one who was supposed to have built the house.

It is always helpful, and a good general practice, to identify the "plaintiff" and the "defendant." This may seem elementary and uncomplicated, but, especially in view of the creative editing practiced by some casebook editors, it is sometimes a difficult or even impossible task. Bear in mind that the *party presently* seeking something from this court may not be the plaintiff, and that sometimes only the cross-claim of a defendant is treated in the excerpt. Confusing or misaligning the parties can ruin your analysis and understanding of the case.

ISSUE: A statement of the general legal question answered by or illustrated in the case. For clarity, the issue is best put in the form of a question capable of a "yes" or "no" answer. In reality, the issue is simply the Rule of Law put in the form of a question (e.g., "May an offer be accepted by performance?").

The major problem presented in discerning what is *the* issue in the case is that an opinion usually purports to raise and answer several questions. However, except for rare cases, only one such question is really the issue in the case. Collateral issues not necessary to the resolution of the matter in controversy are handled by the court by language known as *"obiter dictum"* or merely *"dictum."* While dicta may be included later in the brief, they have no place under the issue heading.

To find the issue, ask *who wants what* and then go on to ask *why did that party succeed or fail in getting it.* Once this is determined, the "why" should be turned into a question.

The complexity of the issues in the cases will vary, but in all cases a single-sentence question should sum up the issue. *In a few cases,* there will be two, or even more rarely, three issues of equal importance to the resolution of the case. Each should be expressed in a single-sentence question.

Since many issues are resolved by a court in coming to a final disposition of a case, the casebook editor will reproduce the portion of the opinion containing the issue or issues most relevant to the area of law under scrutiny. A noted law professor gave this advice: "Close the book; look at the title on the cover." Chances are, if it is Property, you need not concern yourself with whether, for example, the federal government's treatment of the plaintiff's land really raises a federal question sufficient to support jurisdiction on this ground in federal court.

The same rule applies to chapter headings designating sub-areas within the subjects. They tip you off as to what the text is designed to teach. The cases are arranged in a casebook to show a progression or development of the law, so that the preceding cases may also help.

It is also most important to remember to *read the notes and questions* at the end of a case to determine what the editors wanted you to have gleaned from it.

HOLDING AND DECISION: This section should succinctly explain the rationale of the court in arriving at its decision. In capsulizing the "reasoning" of the court, it should always include an application of the general rule or rules of law to the specific facts of the case. Hidden justifications come to light in this entry; the reasons for the state of the law, the public policies, the biases and prejudices, those considerations that influence the justices' thinking and, ultimately, the outcome of the case. At the end, there should be a short indication of the disposition or procedural resolution of the case (e.g., "Decision of the trial court for Mr. Smith (P) reversed").

The foregoing format is designed to help you "digest" the reams of case material with which you will be faced in your law school career. Once mastered by practice, it will place at your fingertips the information the authors of your casebooks have sought to impart to you in case-by-case illustration and analysis.

B. Be as Economical as Possible in Briefing Cases

Once armed with a format that encourages succinctness, it is as important to be economical with regard to the time spent on the actual reading of the case as it is to be economical in the writing of the brief itself. This does not mean "skimming" a case. Rather, it means reading the case with an "eye" trained to recognize into which "section" of your brief a particular passage or line fits and having a system for quickly and precisely marking the case so that the passages fitting any one particular part of

the brief can be easily identified and brought together in a concise and accurate manner when the brief is actually written.

It is of no use to simply repeat everything in the opinion of the court; record only enough information to trigger your recollection of what the court said. Nevertheless, an accurate statement of the "law of the case," i.e., the legal principle applied to the facts, is absolutely essential to class preparation and to learning the law under the case method.

To that end, it is important to develop a "shorthand" that you can use to make margin notations. These notations will tell you at a glance in which section of the brief you will be placing that particular passage or portion of the opinion.

Some students prefer to underline all the salient portions of the opinion (with a pencil or colored underliner marker), making marginal notations as they go along. Others prefer the color-coded method of underlining, utilizing different colors of markers to underline the salient portions of the case, each separate color being used to represent a different section of the brief. For example, blue underlining could be used for passages relating to the rule of law, yellow for those relating to the issue, and green for those relating to the holding and decision, etc. While it has its advocates, the color-coded method can be confusing and time-consuming (all that time spent on changing colored markers). Furthermore, it can interfere with the continuity and concentration many students deem essential to the reading of a case for maximum comprehension. In the end, however, it is a matter of personal preference and style. Just remember, whatever method you use, underlining must be used sparingly or its value is lost.

If you take the marginal notation route, an efficient and easy method is to go along underlining the key portions of the case and placing in the margin alongside them the following "markers" to indicate where a particular passage or line "belongs" in the brief you will write:

N   (NATURE OF CASE)
RL   (RULE OF LAW)
I   (ISSUE)
HL   (HOLDING AND DECISION, relates to the RULE OF LAW behind the decision)
HR   (HOLDING AND DECISION, gives the RATIONALE or reasoning behind the decision)
HA   (HOLDING AND DECISION, APPLIES the general principle(s) of law to the facts of the case to arrive at the decision)

Remember that a particular passage may well contain information necessary to more than one part of your brief, in which case you simply note that in the margin. If you are using the color-coded underlining method instead of margin notation, simply make asterisks or checks in the margin next to the passage in question in the colors that indicate the additional sections of the brief where it might be utilized.

The economy of utilizing "shorthand" in marking cases for briefing can be maintained in the actual brief writing process itself by utilizing "law student shorthand" within the brief. There are many commonly used words and phrases for which abbreviations can be substituted in your briefs (and in your class notes also). You can develop abbreviations that are personal to you and which will save you a lot of time. A reference list of briefing abbreviations can be found on page xii of this book.

C. Use Both the Briefing Process and the Brief as a Learning Tool

Now that you have a format and the tools for briefing cases efficiently, the most important thing is to make the time spent in briefing profitable to you and to make the most advantageous use of the briefs you create. Of course, the briefs are invaluable for classroom reference when you are called upon to explain or analyze a particular

case. However, they are also useful in reviewing for exams. A quick glance at the fact summary should bring the case to mind, and a rereading of the rule of law should enable you to go over the underlying legal concept in your mind, how it was applied in that particular case, and how it might apply in other factual settings.

As to the value to be derived from engaging in the briefing process itself, there is an immediate benefit that arises from being forced to sift through the essential facts and reasoning from the court's opinion and to succinctly express them in your own words in your brief. The process ensures that you understand the case and the point that it illustrates, and that means you will be ready to absorb further analysis and information brought forth in class. It also ensures you will have something to say when called upon in class. The briefing process helps develop a mental agility for getting to the *gist* of a case and for identifying, expounding on, and applying the legal concepts and issues found there. The briefing process is the mental process on which you must rely in taking law school examinations; it is also the mental process upon which a lawyer relies in serving his clients and in making his living.

acceptance	acp	offer	O
affirmed	aff	offeree	OE
answer	ans	offeror	OR
assumption of risk	a/r	ordinance	ord
attorney	atty	pain and suffering	p/s
beyond a reasonable doubt	b/r/d	parol evidence	p/e
bona fide purchaser	BFP	plaintiff	P
breach of contract	br/k	prima facie	p/f
cause of action	c/a	probable cause	p/c
common law	c/l	proximate cause	px/c
Constitution	Con	real property	r/p
constitutional	con	reasonable doubt	r/d
contract	K	reasonable man	r/m
contributory negligence	c/n	rebuttable presumption	rb/p
cross	x	remanded	rem
cross-complaint	x/c	res ipsa loquitur	RIL
cross-examination	x/ex	respondeat superior	r/s
cruel and unusual punishment	c/u/p	Restatement	RS
defendant	D	reversed	rev
dismissed	dis	Rule Against Perpetuities	RAP
double jeopardy	d/j	search and seizure	s/s
due process	d/p	search warrant	s/w
equal protection	e/p	self-defense	s/d
equity	eq	specific performance	s/p
evidence	ev	statute of limitations	S/L
exclude	exc	statute of frauds	S/F
exclusionary rule	exc/r	statute	S
felony	f/n	summary judgment	s/j
freedom of speech	f/s	tenancy in common	t/c
good faith	g/f	tenancy at will	t/w
habeas corpus	h/c	tenant	t
hearsay	hr	third party	TP
husband	H	third party beneficiary	TPB
in loco parentis	ILP	transferred intent	TI
injunction	inj	unconscionable	uncon
inter vivos	I/v	unconstitutional	unconst
joint tenancy	j/t	undue influence	u/e
judgment	judgt	Uniform Commercial Code	UCC
jurisdiction	jur	unilateral	uni
last clear chance	LCC	vendee	VE
long-arm statute	LAS	vendor	VR
majority view	maj	versus	v
meeting of minds	MOM	void for vagueness	VFV
minority view	min	weight of the evidence	w/e
Miranda warnings	Mir/w	weight of authority	w/a
Miranda rule	Mir/r	wife	W
negligence	neg	with	w/
notice	ntc	within	w/i
nuisance	nus	without prejudice	w/o/p
obligation	ob	without	w/o
obscene	obs	wrongful death	wr/d

Table of Cases

Defining the Attorney-Client Relationship

Quick Reference Rules of Law

Perez v. Kirk & Carrigan

Truck driver (P) v. Attorneys (D)

Tex. Ct. App., 822 S.W.2d 261 (1991).

NATURE OF CASE: Appeal from summary judgment in action for breach of fiduciary duty, infliction of emotional distress, and consumer protection violations.

FACT SUMMARY: After Perez's (P) truck accident claimed the lives of twenty-one children, lawyers Kirk & Carrigan (D) disseminated to the district attorney's office the confidential statements he made to them, resulting in Perez's (P) indictment.

🏛 RULE OF LAW
A lawyer may breach his fiduciary duty to his client either by wrongfully disclosing a privileged statement or by disclosing an unprivileged statement after wrongfully representing that it would be kept confidential.

FACTS: Perez (P), a truck driver for the Valley Coca-Cola Bottling Company, was in a traffic accident which resulted in the deaths of twenty-one children. Kirk & Carrigan (D), lawyers hired to represent Valley Coca-Cola Bottling Company, visited Perez (P) the day after the accident in the hospital and told him they were his lawyers too. Perez (P) gave a sworn statement to Kirk & Carrigan (D) with the understanding that the statement would be kept confidential. Soon thereafter, Kirk & Carrigan (D) voluntarily disclosed Perez's (P) statement to the district attorney's office under threat of subpoena. The district attorney's office obtained an indictment for involuntary manslaughter against Perez (P) based upon the statement. Perez (P) brought an action for breach of fiduciary duty against Kirk & Carrigan (D). Kirk & Carrigan (D) moved for summary judgment on the ground that the attorney-client privilege did not apply to Perez's (P) statement. The trial court granted summary judgment, and Perez (P) appealed.

ISSUE: Does a lawyer breach his fiduciary duty to maintain his client's confidences by disclosing an unprivileged statement after representing that it would be kept confidential?

HOLDING AND DECISION: (Dorsey, J.) Yes. A lawyer breaches his fiduciary duty to maintain his client's confidences by disclosing an unprivileged statement after representing that it would be kept confidential. Perez's (P) allegation here that Kirk & Carrigan (D) breached their fiduciary duty owed to him when they voluntarily disseminated his statement to the district attorney's office was a valid claim for damages for the emotional distress and mental anguish he suffered after being indicted. Once an attorney-client relationship arose between Kirk & Carrigan (D) and Perez (P), Kirk & Carigan (D) had a fiduciary and ethical duty not to disseminate statements Perez (P) made to them in confidence, regardless of whether the statements were privileged or not. The relationship between attorney and client requires absolute and perfect candor, openness and honesty, and the absence of any concealment or deception. Perez (P) has made a valid claim for damages. Reversed and remanded.

▶ ANALYSIS

It is important to note that much information that is ethically protected will not be privileged. However, virtually all information considered privileged under the Rules of Evidence will also be ethically protected. A lawyer whom a court orders to reveal information that is ethically protected but not privileged under the Rules of Evidence will be required to reveal the information under pain of contempt. But if that lawyer had voluntarily revealed the same information, he or she might be guilty of a disciplinary violation for failure to protect a client's secrets or confidences, unless revelation was for one of the purposes recognized by DR 4-101 or Rule 1.6.

■=■

Quicknotes

ATTORNEY-CLIENT PRIVILEGE A doctrine precluding the admission into evidence of confidential communications between an attorney and his client made in the course of obtaining professional assistance.

FIDUCIARY DUTY A legal obligation to act for the benefit of another, including subordinating one's personal interests to that of the other person.

■=■

Upjohn Co. v. United States

Audited corporation (D) v. Internal Revenue Service (P)

449 U.S. 383 (1981).

NATURE OF CASE: Review of discovery order in tax investigation.

FACT SUMMARY: The Internal Revenue Service (IRS) (P), in a tax investigation of Upjohn Co. (D), sought disclosure of communications between middle- and lower-level employees and Upjohn's (D) attorneys.

RULE OF LAW
The attorney-client privilege between a corporation and its counsel extends to communications between counsel and noncontrol-level employees.

FACTS: The IRS (P), in the course of a tax investigation of Upjohn Co. (D), sought disclosure of memoranda compiled by corporate attorneys during the course of their communications with nonsupervisory personnel. Upjohn (D) resisted, claiming the attorney-client privilege. The court of appeals held that the privilege applied only to communications between counsel and "control" employees, such as executives and senior management. The Supreme Court granted review.

ISSUE: Does the attorney-client privilege between a corporation and its counsel extend to communications between counsel and noncontrol-level employees?

HOLDING AND DECISION: (Rehnquist, J.) Yes. The attorney-client privilege between a corporation and its counsel extends to communications between counsel and noncontrol-level employees. The privilege exists largely because of a recognition in the law that sound legal advice depends upon the lawyer being fully informed of relevant facts; if communications between a client and his counsel were discoverable, such communication would be largely circumscribed. In the context of a corporation, the information necessary for the corporation's attorneys to properly represent the corporation will not always come from the corporation's "control group," often, the information will be in the possession of midlevel or even low-level employees. Communications between such employees and counsel may be no less necessary for proper representation, and therefore are no less deserving of confidentiality. Therefore, the privilege must be extended to all communications between counsel and corporate employees, no matter what level. Reversed.

ANALYSIS

It is important to note that the attorney-client privilege protects communications only, not information. While an attorney may not be compelled to disclose what a corporate attorney communicated to him, the privilege does not bar the party seeking discovery from obtaining the information from the employee through a recognized discovery procedure such as a deposition. While it would be more convenient for the IRS (P), for example, to simply subpoena the notes taken by Upjohn's (D) attorney, the court notes that considerations of convenience do not overcome the policies served by the attorney-client privilege.

■■■

Quicknotes

ATTORNEY-CLIENT PRIVILEGE A doctrine precluding the admission into evidence of confidential communications between an attorney and his client made in the course of obtaining professional assistance.

■■■

Samaritan Foundation v. Goodfarb

Hospital (D) v. Injured child (P)

Ariz. Sup. Ct., 862 P.2d 870 (1993).

NATURE OF CASE: Motion for production in medical negligence action

FACT SUMMARY: A lawyer representing a child (P) in a medical negligence action against Phoenix Children's Hospital in the Good Samaritan Regional Medical Center (Hospital) (D) made a discovery request for employee interview summaries prepared by the Hospital (D) paralegal at the request of the Hospital's (D) corporate counsel, who argued that the interview summaries were protected under attorney-client privilege.

🏛 RULE OF LAW
An employee's communications to corporate counsel are within the corporation's privilege if they concern the employee's own conduct within the scope of her employment and are made to assist the lawyer in assessing the legal consequences of that conduct for the corporation.

FACTS: A child's (P) heart stopped during surgery, and the child (P) and her parents (P) brought an action in medical negligence against Phoenix Children's Hospital in the Good Samaritan Regional Medical Center (Hospital) (D). The Hospital's (D) corporate counsel directed a nurse paralegal to interview three nurses and a scrub technician present during the surgery and to summarize the interviews in memoranda. Two years later, when the child's (P) attorney made a discovery request for the interview summaries, the Hospital's (D) corporate counsel resisted by arguing that the interview summaries were protected by the attorney-client privilege and the work-product doctrine.

ISSUE: Does the corporate attorney-client privilege apply to all corporate employee communications made to counsel?

HOLDING AND DECISION: (Martone, J.) No. An employee's communications to corporate counsel are within the corporation's privilege only if they concern the employee's own conduct within the scope of her employment and are made to assist the lawyer in assessing the legal consequences of that conduct for the corporation. Here, the statements made by the nurses and the scrub technician were not within the corporate attorney-client privilege because these employees were not seeking legal advice in confidence. Since their actions did not subject the Hospital (D) to potential liability, their statements were not gathered to assist the Hospital (D) in assessing or responding to the legal consequences of the speaker's conduct. They were employee-witnesses, not employee-clients. Therefore, their statements are discoverable.

▶ ANALYSIS

The purpose of the holding in this case is to provide courts with the means of determining which communications made by the corporation's agents are those of the corporate client and not merely those of the individual speaker. While the corporate entity can only act through its agents, client communications cannot be identified simply as those of particular agents. By considering factors such as confidentiality and potential liability of the corporate client, the court seeks to avoid frustrating the very purpose of the privilege by discouraging the communication of relevant information by employees of the client to attorneys seeking to render legal advice to the client corporation.

■■■

Quicknotes

ATTORNEY-CLIENT PRIVILEGE A doctrine precluding the admission into evidence of confidential communications between an attorney and his client made in the course of obtaining professional assistance.

WORK PRODUCT Work performed by an attorney in preparation of litigation that is not subject to discovery.

■■■

Taylor v. Illinois

Convicted criminal (D) v. Illinois (P)

484 U.S. 400 (1988).

NATURE OF CASE: Appeal from a criminal conviction.

FACT SUMMARY: Taylor (D) received a criminal conviction after the court refused to allow him to call a critical witness because his defense lawyer had failed to provide the prosecutor for the State of Illinois (P) with the name of the witness.

▥ RULE OF LAW
The client must accept the consequences of the lawyer's decision to forgo cross-examination, to not put certain witnesses on the stand, or to not disclose the identity of certain witnesses in advance of trial.

FACTS: When Taylor's (D) lawyer refused to comply with the state prosecutor's (P) discovery request for the name of a witness pursuant to Illinois (P) discovery rules, the trial court judge refused to allow Taylor's (D) lawyer to call the witness whose testimony would have helped establish a defense of self-defense during the trial. Taylor (D) was convicted. Taylor's (D) conviction was upheld by the Illinois appellate courts, and Taylor (D) appealed to the U.S. Supreme Court, arguing that he should not be held responsible for his lawyer's misconduct.

ISSUE: When a lawyer decides to forgo cross-examination, to not put certain witnesses on the stand, or to not disclose the identity of certain witnesses in advance of trial, must a client accept the consequences of the lawyer's decision?

HOLDING AND DECISION: (Stevens, J.) Yes. The client must accept the consequences of the lawyer's decision to forgo cross-examination, to not put certain witnesses on the stand, or to not disclose the identity of certain witnesses in advance of trial. Taylor's (D) lawyer chose not to reveal his witness's identity until after the trial commenced. Taylor (D) has no right to disavow that decision now, absent ineffective assistance of counsel. Moreover, in responding to discovery, the client has a duty to be candid and forthcoming with the lawyer, and when the lawyer responds, he speaks for the client.

DISSENT: (Brennan, J.) In the absence of any evidence that a defendant played any part in an attorney's willful discovery violation, directly sanctioning the attorney is not only fairer but more effective in deterring violations than excluding defense evidence. While the court has sometimes held a defendant bound by tactical errors his attorney makes, we have not previously suggested that a client can be punished for an attorney's misconduct. There is no need to inflict punishment on the defendant because misconduct, not tactical errors, is amenable to direct punitive sanctions against attorneys as a deterrent that can prevent attorneys from systematically engaging in misconduct that would disrupt the trial process.

▶ ANALYSIS

This case stands for the proposition that lawyers are their clients' agents. As such, the lawyer must have full authority to manage the conduct of his client's case because it would be impracticable to require client approval of every tactical decision a lawyer may make. Consequently, the lawyer's conduct will be attributable to the client, even if the lawyer errs or is careless.

Quicknotes

ATTORNEY-CLIENT PRIVILEGE A doctrine precluding the admission into evidence of confidential communications between an attorney and his client made in the course of obtaining professional assistance.

INEFFECTIVE ASSISTANCE OF COUNSEL A claim brought by an accused in which it must be determined whether the attorney's rendering of representation was such that the ultimate disposition of the case may not be relied upon as fair.

S.E.C. v. McNulty

Federal agency (P) v. Corporate insider (D)

137 F.3d 732 (2d Cir. 1998).

NATURE OF CASE: Appeal from default judgment in action for securities fraud.

FACT SUMMARY: Shanklin (D) contended that the willful failure of his attorney, Rucker, to file an answer to a complaint filed against him by the Securities and Exchange Commission (SEC) (P) should not have been imputed to him, so that a default judgment entered against him should have been vacated.

🏛 RULE OF LAW
An attorney's willful default will be imputed to the attorney's client where the client is a sophisticated business person and has failed to monitor the attorney's efforts on his behalf.

FACTS: The Securities and Exchange Commission (SEC) (P) filed a complaint against Shanklin (D), a sophisticated business person, alleging that he knew, or recklessly failed to know, of securities fraud committed by McNulty (D). Shanklin's (D) attorney, Rucker, neglected to file an answer to the complaint, and a default judgment was entered against Shanklin (D). Shanklin (D) had failed to contact Ruker (D) for over a year about filing an answer. Shanklin (D) moved to vacate the default judgment, but the district court ruled that he had failed to demonstrate that the default was not willful since Rucker's conduct had been egregious, and more than merely negligent, or even grossly negligent. Shanklin (D) appealed, arguing that Rucker's conduct should not have been imputed to him, and the Court of Appeals granted review.

ISSUE: Will an attorney's willful default be imputed to the attorney's client where the client is a sophisticated business person and has failed to monitor the attorney's efforts on his behalf?

HOLDING AND DECISION: (Kearse, J.) Yes. An attorney's willful default will be imputed to the attorney's client where the client is a sophisticated business person and has failed to monitor the attorney's efforts on his behalf. First, the record amply supports the district court's finding that Rucker's conduct was egregious, i.e., more than merely negligent or grossly negligent, and, that, therefore, it was willful. The question then becomes whether such willfulness can be imputed to Shanklin (D). In our system of representative litigation, the conduct of an attorney is normally imputed to the attorney's client, since permitting the client to evade the consequences of the acts or omissions of his freely selected agent, the attorney, would undermine that system. There was no evidence that Shanklin (D), a sophisticated businessman, ever made any

efforts to determine whether Rucker was tending to the lawsuit before the default occurred, despite not receiving any bills or other communications from Rucker during the year between the time Rucker was retained and the time the default was entered. It is not enough that Shanklin (D) has been diligent in attempting to reverse the consequences of Rucker's "outrageous incompetence" since the default judgment has been entered. Accordingly, Rucker's willful default must be imputed to Shanklin (D). Affirmed.

▶ ANALYSIS

In our adversarial litigation system, each party is deemed bound by the acts of his lawyer-agent. Thus, while the attorney's improper conduct may bind the client, the client's recourse is to sue the attorney for damages in a separate legal malpractice action.

Quicknotes

DEFAULT JUDGMENT A judgment entered against a defendant due to his failure to appear in a court or defend himself against the allegations of the opposing party.

GROSS NEGLIGENCE The intentional failure to perform a duty with reckless disregard of the consequences.

IMPUTED NEGLIGENCE The assignment of negligence liability from one person or legal entity to another based on the relationship between the two.

LEGAL MALPRACTICE Conduct on the part of an attorney falling below that demonstrated by other attorneys of ordinary skill and competency under the circumstances, resulting in damages.

NEGLIGENCE Conduct falling below the standard of care that a reasonable person would demonstrate under similar conditions.

Nichols v. Keller

Injured employee (P) v. Workers' compensation attorneys (D)

Cal. App. Ct., 15 Cal. App. 4th 1672, 19 Cal. Rptr. 2d 601 (1993).

NATURE OF CASE: Appeal from summary judgment dismissing malpractice action.

FACT SUMMARY: Fulfer & Keller (D) contended that they had not been obligated to advise client Nichols (P) of his civil suit remedies following a work-related injury because they represented him only on his workers' compensation claim.

🏛 RULE OF LAW
An attorney may be obligated to alert a client to legal remedies outside the direct scope of that attorney's representation of the client.

FACTS: Nichols (P) suffered a job-related injury. He retained Fulfer & Keller (D) to represent him in a workers' compensation claim. He did not learn of his potential recourse against third parties by way of civil suit until after the statute of limitations had passed. He sued Fulfer & Keller (D) for malpractice, contending that they had been under a duty to advise him of his rights with respect to a third-party suit. The trial court granted summary judgment dismissing the action, holding that Fulfer & Keller (D) did not owe him any such duty as it was not within the course of their representation. Nichols (P) appealed.

ISSUE: May an attorney be obligated to alert a client to legal remedies outside the direct scope of that attorney's representation of the client?

HOLDING AND DECISION: [Judge not stated in casebook excerpt.] Yes. An attorney may be obligated to alert a client to legal remedies outside the direct scope of that attorney's representation of the client. One of the attorney's basic functions is to advise. Advice need not be on every possible alternative, but should cover all foreseeable negative consequences. If such a consequence is foreseeable even in an area outside the attorney's scope of representation, the attorney is still under a duty to disclose the risk. He can then advise the client that it is outside his expertise and/or scope of representation and that the client should seek other counsel, and then the onus is placed on the client to protect his rights. However, until this is done, it is the attorney's responsibility to inform the client of such rights. Here, even though Fulfer & Keller (D) represented Nichols (P) only on his workers' compensation claim, a civil suit was sufficiently related to the scope of the representation that Nichols (P) should at least have been advised that the remedy existed. Reversed.

▶ ANALYSIS

If there is one thing that gets lawyers in trouble with clients, it is lack of communication. Generally speaking, a

lawyer can never disclose too much to a client; he can, however, disclose too little, with consequences of the sort seen here. A good rule of thumb is "when in doubt, disclose."

■■■

Quicknotes

DUTY OF CARE A principle of negligence requiring an individual to act in such a manner as to avoid injury to a person to whom he or she owes an obligatory duty.

STATUTE OF LIMITATIONS A law prescribing the period in which a legal action may be commenced.

■■■

Jones v. Barnes

Public defender (D) v. Convicted robber (P)

463 U.S. 745 (1983).

NATURE OF CASE: Review of grant of habeas corpus.

FACT SUMMARY: Barnes (D) contended that he had an absolute right to have his attorney on appeal raise every nonfrivolous issue he requested.

RULE OF LAW
An attorney representing a defendant on appeal is not under a duty to raise every nonfrivolous issue requested by the defendant.

FACTS: Barnes (P) was convicted of armed robbery. A public defender was appointed to prosecute his appeal. Barnes (P) requested that certain issues be raised in the appeal. The attorney, for reasons of strategy, declined to press all the proffered issues. The conviction was affirmed. Barnes (P) petitioned for habeas corpus, contending that his attorney's refusal to prosecute all nonfrivolous issues constituted a denial of his Sixth Amendment right to counsel. The Second Circuit granted the writ, and the Supreme Court granted review.

ISSUE: Is an attorney representing a defendant on appeal under a duty to raise every nonfrivolous issue requested by the defendant?

HOLDING AND DECISION: (Burger, C.J.) No. An attorney representing a defendant on appeal is not under a duty to raise every nonfrivolous issue requested by the defendant. It is safe to assume that counsel is in a better position than the defendant to assess how best to prosecute an appeal. In many situations, raising every issue will be detrimental to an appeal, as the weaker points will drown the stronger ones. To create a per se rule that a defendant is entitled to have appointed counsel raise every issue he wishes would seriously undermine the ability of counsel to present the client's case in accord with counsel's professional judgment. This Court is unwilling to take such a step. Reversed.

CONCURRENCE: (Blackmun, J.) An attorney may be ethically bound to raise all nonfrivolous issues requested by the client, but this duty does not rise to constitutional status.

DISSENT: Brennan, J.) An appeal ultimately belongs to the defendant, and he must have the final say in how it is prosecuted.

ANALYSIS

It must be remembered that this was a constitutional ruling. The Court simply held that, as a matter of federal constitutional law, no right to press all issues on appeal belongs to one having appointed counsel. Depending on jurisdiction, an attorney may have an ethical obligation to prosecute all such issues. Canon 5 of the ABA Code of Professional Responsibility concerns an attorney's obligation to exercise independent professional judgment on behalf of such a client. This canon is primarily concerned with avoiding external, third-party influences over the attorney's decision-making process. It does not speak to interference by the client himself.

Quicknotes

HABEAS CORPUS A proceeding in which a defendant brings a writ to compel a judicial determination of whether he is lawfully being held in custody.

Olfe v. Gordon

Property seller (P) v. Real estate attorney (D)

Wis. Sup. Ct., 93 Wis. 2d 173, 286 N.W.2d 573 (1980).

NATURE OF CASE: Appeal of dismissal of action against an attorney by his former client.

FACT SUMMARY: A trial court held that expert testimony was required for Olfe (P) to recover against her former attorney, Gordon (D), even though he had intentionally disregarded her instructions in the underlying transaction.

🏛 RULE OF LAW
When an attorney disregards a client's instructions to the client's detriment, expert testimony is not required for the client to recover.

FACTS: Olfe (P) retained Gordon (D), an attorney, to handle the sale of her house. She instructed him that she was willing to take back a first mortgage, but not a second mortgage. Nonetheless, Gordon (D) arranged a transaction which left Olfe (P) with a second mortgage, although Gordon (D) told her it was in fact a first mortgage. The purchaser defaulted, and the holder of the first mortgage foreclosed, extinguishing Olfe's (P) second mortgage. Olfe (P) lost about $25,000, and sued Gordon (D) to recover. After Olfe's (P) case, the court granted a nonsuit, on the basis that Olfe (P) had not provided expert testimony as to the standard of care required by attorneys in similar circumstances. Olfe (P) appealed.

ISSUE: When an attorney disregards a client's instructions to the client's detriment, is expert testimony required for the client to recover?

HOLDING AND DECISION: [Judge not stated in casebook excerpt.] No. When an attorney disregards a client's instructions to the detriment of the client, expert testimony is not required for the client to recover. It has generally been recognized that an attorney may be liable for all losses caused by his failure to follow with reasonable promptness and care the explicit instructions of his client. Moreover, an attorney's honest belief that the instructions were not in the best interests of the client provides no defense to a suit for malpractice. The attorney-client relationship in such contexts is one of agent to principal, and an agent is answerable to that principal for failure to follow instructions. A cause of action in this situation may be based upon fiduciary principles, upon contract, or in tort. In any event, expert testimony is not needed, as a lay jury is perfectly capable of understanding on its own whether an attorney failed to follow instructions. Reversed.

▶ ANALYSIS

The ABA Code of professional responsibility does not say in so many words that an attorney is duty-bound to follow his client's instructions. Canon 7 does require an attorney to represent a client zealously, but no mandate regarding instructions is made. The rule here is more a product of agency law than the code of ethics.

Quicknotes

DUTY OF CARE A principle of negligence requiring an individual to act in such a manner as to avoid injury to a person to whom he or she owes an obligatory duty.

Protecting the Attorney-Client Relationship Against Invasion

Quick Reference Rules of Law

Niesig v. Team I

Injured construction worker (P) v. Unidentified (D)

N.Y. Ct. App., 76 N.Y.2d 363, 558 N.E.2d 1030, 559 N.Y.S.2d 493 (1990).

NATURE OF CASE: Appeal of ruling on motion to permit ex parte interviews.

FACT SUMMARY: Niesig's (P) attorney wished to conduct interviews with employees of De Trae Enterprises, Inc. (D) without the presence of De Trae's (D) counsel.

🏛 RULE OF LAW
An attorney may conduct ex parte interviews with a corporate adversary's employees if the employees do not have power to bind the corporation.

FACTS: Niesig (P) was injured on a construction site. He sued various entities. Joined as a third-party defendant was his employer, De Trae Enterprises, Inc. (D). Niesig's (P) attorney, wishing to conduct ex parte interviews with De Trae (D) employee-witnesses, moved the court for an order approving such action. [The casebook excerpt did not state the trial court ruling.] The appellate division held that current employees were "parties" and therefore could not be communicated with directly. The New York Court of Appeals granted review.

ISSUE: May an attorney conduct ex parte interviews with a corporate adversary's employees if the employees do not have power to bind the corporation?

HOLDING AND DECISION: (Kaye, J.) Yes. An attorney may conduct ex parte interviews with a corporate adversary's employees if the employees do not have power to bind the corporation. DR 7104(A)(1) of the New York Code of Professional Responsibility contains the universal prohibition against communicating with opposing "parties." When opponents are corporations, the question arises as to who will be considered a "party," as a corporation can only act through individuals. As the Code of Professional Responsibility is not a statute, this court does not have to give effect to any legislative intent and can interpret the rule as it sees fit. One interpretation urged, which this court rejects, would hold all employees to be covered. This is unsatisfactory because it would preclude informal discovery, which is an expedient way of helping to resolve disputes. Another interpretation would be the so-called "control group" test, which holds that only controlling individuals in a corporation (usually executives) would be covered by the rule. This rule wholly overlooks the fact that corporate employees other than senior management can speak for a corporation. The best rule, in this court's view, is one that includes all persons who have authority to bind the corporation. This test will not be hard to apply, as it is grounded in principles of agency and evidence which are well known to attorneys. This rule is

different than the one issued by the appellate division, so its order is modified and the matter remanded.

CONCURRENCE: (Bellacosa, J.) The "control group" test is preferable because it better balances the parties' interests in allowing maximum information-gathering while still safeguarding attorney protections for those individuals vital to a corporation.

▶ ANALYSIS

The court here partially based its decision upon rules of evidence, although it did not specify the rules to which it was referring. In fact, at least at the federal level, evidentiary rules are different. For instance, the attorney-client privilege applies to all employees, not just "alter ego" employees.

■=■

Quicknotes

ATTORNEY-CLIENT PRIVILEGE A doctrine precluding the admission into evidence of confidential communications between an attorney and his client made in the course of obtaining professional assistance.

EX PARTE A proceeding commenced by one party without providing any opposing parties with notice or which is uncontested by an adverse party.

NEW YORK CODE OF PROFESSIONAL RESPONSIBILITY DR 7-104(A)(1) Prohibits a lawyer from communicating directly with a party known to have counsel in the matter.

■=■

United States v. Hammad

Federal government (P) v. Department store owners (D)

858 F.2d 834 (2d Cir. 1988), *cert. denied*, 498 U.S. 871 (1990).

NATURE OF CASE: Interlocutory appeal of order excluding evidence in a criminal prosecution.

FACT SUMMARY: A Government (P) informant obtained incriminating statements from Hammad (D) during a meeting, although Hammad (D) had already retained counsel.

🏛 RULE OF LAW
Prosecutors may use informants to meet with subjects of criminal investigations, even if they are known to have counsel, in pre-indictment noncustodial situations.

FACTS: Hammad (D) became the focus of a government (P) fraud and conspiracy investigation. The Government (P) coerced Goldstein, an associate of Hammad (D), to meet with Hammad (D) to discuss a fictitious subpoena supposedly requiring Goldstein to testify regarding Hammad's (D) activities. The Government (P) knew that Hammad (D) had counsel. The meeting took place, and Hammad (D) made incriminating statements that Goldstein secretly recorded. Indicted for various felonies, Hammad (D) moved to suppress the evidence. He argued that the Government (P) had violated DR 7-104(A)(1), the prohibition against communications by counsel with represented adversaries. The district court suppressed the evidence and the Government (P) made an interlocutory appeal.

ISSUE: In pre-indictment, noncustodial situations, may prosecutors use informants to meet with subjects of criminal investigations even if they are known to have counsel?

HOLDING AND DECISION: (Kaufman, J.) Yes. In pre-indictment, noncustodial situations, prosecutors may use informants to meet with subjects of criminal investigations even if they are known to have counsel. Under DR 7-104(A)(1), a prosecutor is authorized by law to employ legitimate investigative techniques in conducting criminal investigations. The use of informants will generally fall within the ambit of such authorization, so any prohibition that 7-104(A)(1) might otherwise place on the use of informants is otherwise nullified. [The court went on to hold that the use of fraudulent subpoenas was a misuse of court process and did not fall within the "authorized by law" exception to 7-104(A)(1). Nonetheless, it reversed the district court's suppression order, finding it to have been an abuse of discretion under the facts of the case and holding that the present decision would have prospective effect only.]

▶ ANALYSIS

The Sixth Amendment's right to counsel provisions only attach after indictment. The Government (P) therefore argued that DR 7-104(A)(1) was inapplicable to pre-indictment proceedings such as those at issue here. The court disagreed. The Sixth Amendment, noted the court, was a minimum standard of conduct below which the prosecutors could not fall. The code of ethics aimed higher and was, therefore, not coextensive with the Constitution.

■═■

Quicknotes

EXCLUSIONARY RULE A rule precluding the introduction at trial of evidence unlawfully obtained in violation of the federal constitutional safeguards against unreasonable searches and seizures.

NEW YORK CODE OF PROFESSIONAL RESPONSIBILITY DR 7-104(A)(1) Authorizes a prosecutor to employ legitimate investigating techniques in conducting criminal investigations which may frequently include informants.

■═■

Rico v. Mitsubishi Motors Corp.

Auto accident victim (P) v. Automobile manufacturer (D)

Cal. Sup. Ct., 42 Cal. 4th 807, 171 P.3d 1092, 68 Cal. Rptr. 3d 758 (2007).

NATURE OF CASE: Appeal from affirmance of order disqualifying plaintiffs' attorneys and experts.

FACT SUMMARY: The plaintiffs (P) in a case involving a rolled-over vehicle manufactured by Mitsubishi Motors Corp. (D) contended that their attorneys and experts should not have been disqualified when their attorney, Johnson, inadvertently received privileged work product belonging to Yukevich, Mitsubishi's (D) counsel, distributed copies of it to his co-counsel and experts, and used it against an expert for the defense at a deposition.

🏛 RULE OF LAW

(1) When a lawyer who receives materials that obviously appear to be subject to an attorney-client privilege or otherwise clearly appear to be confidential and privileged and where it is reasonably apparent that the materials were provided or made available through inadvertence, the lawyer receiving such materials should refrain from examining the materials any more than is essential to ascertain if the materials are privileged, and must immediately notify the materials' originator that he or she possesses material that appears to be privileged.

(2) Disqualification of a party's attorneys and experts is appropriate where they have obtained and used an adversary's privileged work product in violation of rules of ethics, and such use is irremediably prejudicial to the adversary.

FACTS: Various plaintiffs (P) brought suit against Mitsubishi Motors Corp. (D) and the state's department of transportation (Caltrans) (D) after a vehicle manufactured by Mitsubishi (D) rolled over on a freeway. Mitsubishi (D) representatives met with their lawyers, Yukevich and Calfo, to discuss their defense strategy. Yukevich had notes from the meeting typed on his computer and never showed the notes to anyone. The notes' sole purpose was to assist Yukevich in defending the case. Less than two weeks after this meeting, Yukevich deposed one of plaintiffs' (P) expert witnesses. At some point, only plaintiffs' (P) counsel, Johnson, and plaintiffs' (P) representative were in the room, where Yukevich had left his case file, which contained the strategy meeting notes. Somehow, Johnson obtained these notes. Yukevich maintained that Johnson had taken the notes from his file, but Johnson maintained that he had been given the notes by the court reporter. The trial court held a hearing on the matter and determined that Johnson had obtained the notes through inadvertence. Johnson admitted that after a minute or two of review he realized the notes related to the case and that

Yukevich did not intend to reveal them. Notwithstanding this realization, Johnson made a copy of the notes, and distributed them to his co-counsel and his experts, all of whom studied and discussed them. Then Johnson used the notes to impeach a defense expert at a deposition. The notes were not revealed until after the deposition, at which point Yukevich realized that Johnson had his only copy of the strategy session notes. Yukevich immediately demanded the return of the notes and all duplicates, and moved to disqualify the plaintiffs' (P) legal team and experts on the grounds that they had become privy to and had used Yukevich's work product, and that such use irremediably prejudiced Mitsubishi (D) and Caltrans (D). The trial court concluded that the notes were absolutely privileged by the work product rule and that Johnson's conduct had been unethical. Because it also agreed that such conduct had irremediably prejudiced the defendants (D), the court disqualified attorneys and experts. The state's intermediate appellate court affirmed, and the state's highest court granted review.

ISSUE:
(1) When a lawyer who receives materials that obviously appear to be subject to an attorney-client privilege or otherwise clearly appear to be confidential and privileged and where it is reasonably apparent that the materials were provided or made available through inadvertence, should the lawyer receiving such materials refrain from examining the materials any more than is essential to ascertain if the materials are privileged, and must the lawyer immediately notify the materials' originator that he or she possesses material that appears to be privileged?

(2) Is disqualification of a party's attorneys and experts appropriate where they have obtained and used an adversary's privileged work product in violation of rules of ethics, and such use is irremediably prejudicial to the adversary?

HOLDING AND DECISION: (Corrigan, J.)
(1) Yes. When a lawyer who receives materials that obviously appear to be subject to an attorney-client privilege or otherwise clearly appear to be confidential and privileged and where it is reasonably apparent that the materials were provided or made available through inadvertence, the lawyer receiving such materials should refrain from examining the materials any more than is essential to ascertain if the materials are privileged, and must immediately notify the materials' originator that he or she possesses material that appears to be privileged. First, the plaintiffs' (P) reliance on a case where the inadvertently received work product was not privileged

Continued on next page.

and its use was not prejudicial is inapposite, since here the work product was absolutely privileged and prejudiced Mitsubishi (D) and Caltrans (D). Moreover, the state's case law makes clear that when a lawyer inadvertently receives materials that are obviously subject to an attorney-client privilege or are confidential and privileged, the lawyer has an ethical obligation to refrain from examining the materials any more than is essential to ascertain if the materials are privileged, and must immediately notify the materials' originator that he or she possesses the privileged or confidential materials. The parties may then proceed to resolve the situation by agreement or may resort to the court for guidance with the benefit of protective orders and other judicial intervention as may be justified. This approach is fair and reasonable, and supports the work product doctrine in the context of discovery that potentially requires the production of massive numbers of documents. It also is consonant with an attorney's obligation not only to protect his client's interests, but also those of fellow members of the bar, the judiciary, and the administration of justice. Applying this standard here, it is clear that they were privileged, even though the strategy meeting notes were not marked as confidential; Johnson's own admission to this effect confirms that he violated his obligations when he somehow obtained the notes. Affirmed as to this issue.

(2) Yes. Disqualification of a party's attorneys and experts is appropriate where they have obtained and used an adversary's privileged work product in violation of rules of ethics, and such use is irremediably prejudicial to the adversary. Mere exposure to an adversary's confidences is insufficient, standing alone, to warrant an attorney's disqualification. Nevertheless, disqualification may be appropriate where the inadvertent recipient of the work product does not conform his or her conduct to ethical strictures mandated by law. Here, Johnson's dissemination of the notes was unethical, as was his use of them to impeach the defense's expert. Because such unethical conduct resulted in irreversible damage to Mitsubishi (D) and Caltrans (D), the lower courts did not abuse their discretion in concluding that disqualification was appropriate, since otherwise the defendants (D) would be at a great disadvantage. Affirmed as to this issue.

▶ ANALYSIS

The rule that an attorney who inadvertently receives materials that are clearly work product must refrain from examining the materials any more than is essential to ascertain if the materials are privileged, and must immediately notify the materials' originator that he or she possesses material that appears to be privileged, is an objective standard. This means that in applying the rule, courts must consider whether reasonably competent counsel, knowing the circumstances of the litigation, would have concluded the materials were pri-

vileged, how much review was reasonably necessary to draw that conclusion, and when counsel's examination should have ended. The rule also supports modern discovery, since the party responding to a request for mass production must engage in a laborious, time consuming process. If the document producer is confronted with the additional prospect that any privileged documents inadvertently produced will become fair game for the opposition, the minute screening and re-screening that inevitably would follow not only would add enormously to that burden but would slow the pace of discovery to a degree sharply at odds with the general goal of expediting litigation. The rule thus avoids inadvertent waiver of the work product privilege in an environment where even the most careful attorney may inadvertently provide protected materials to an opponent.

■═■

Quicknotes

ATTORNEY-CLIENT PRIVILEGE A doctrine precluding the admission into evidence of confidential communications between an attorney and his client made in the course of obtaining professional assistance.

DEPOSITION A pretrial discovery procedure whereby oral or written questions are asked by one party of the opposing party or of a witness for the opposing party under oath in preparation for litigation.

EXPERT WITNESS A witness providing testimony at trial who is specially qualified regarding the particular subject matter involved.

IMPEACHMENT The discrediting of a witness by offering evidence to show that the witness lacks credibility.

■═■

CHAPTER 4

Lawyers, Money, and the Ethics of Legal Fees

Quick Reference Rules of Law

Brobeck, Phleger & Harrison v. Telex Corp.

Law firm (P) v. Computer corporation (D)

602 F.2d 866 (9th Cir.), *cert. denied*, 444 U.S. 981 (1979).

NATURE OF CASE: Appeal of award of damages for breach of contract.

FACT SUMMARY: Telex Corp. (D) contended that a contingency fee of $1,000,000 for the handling of a writ of certiorari to the Supreme Court was unconscionable.

🏛 RULE OF LAW
A contingency fee of $1,000,000 for handling a writ of certiorari to the Supreme Court is not unconscionable.

FACTS: Telex Corp. (D) filed an antitrust action against International Business Machines, Inc. It recovered $259,000,000, but IBM recovered $18,500,000 by way of counterclaim. On appeal, the court of appeals reversed Telex's (D) award but affirmed that of IBM. Telex (D) engaged the firm of Brobeck, Phleger & Harrison (Brobeck) (P), a preeminent antitrust litigation firm, to handle a writ of certiorari to the Supreme Court. The fee arrangement called for a $25,000 retainer with a 5% contingency provision, the contingency in no event to be less than $1,000,000 in the event of a successful conclusion. [Telex (D) later denied that this had been the arrangement.] The petition was filed. Brobeck (P) eventually worked out a "wash" settlement wherein the writ would be dismissed in exchange for a dismissal of the counterclaim. Brobeck (P) then submitted a bill for $1,000,000, which Telex (D) refused to pay. Brobeck (P) sued for breach of contract. The district court awarded $1,000,000. Telex (D) appealed, contending (1) that the amount awarded did not reflect the terms of the contract, and (2) the amount of the contract was unconscionable.

ISSUE: Is a contingency fee of $1,000,000 for handling a writ of certiorari to the Supreme Court unconscionable?

HOLDING AND DECISION: (Per curiam) No. A contingency fee of $1,000,000 for handling a writ of certiorari to the Supreme Court is not unconscionable. [The Court first decided that the award did in fact reflect the terms of the contract.] A contract will be unconscionable only if it is one that "no man in his senses and not under a delusion would make on the one hand, and no honest man would accept on the other." Such an analysis will naturally depend on the facts of the case. In this particular instance, the client, Telex (D), was faced with a large judgment which apparently jeopardized its continued corporate existence. It engaged the services of a high-profile law firm, whose engagement was almost surely one of the reasons IBM was willing to dismiss its judgment in exchange for a dismissal of the certiorari petition. Under these circumstances, the retainer agreement cannot be said to fall within the test above. This is particularly true in light of the fact that Telex (D) in no way could have been considered an unsophisticated client. Affirmed.

▶ ANALYSIS

DR 2-106 of the ABA code of professional responsibility provides, "A lawyer shall not enter into an agreement for, charge, or collect an illegal or clearly excessive fee." The Rule goes on to list certain factors to be considered in determining whether a fee is clearly excessive. Of particular importance was the factor enumerated in DR 2-106(B)(7): "[T]he experience, reputation, and ability of the lawyer or lawyers performing the services." In this instance, Telex (D) wanted and got the best, and for that it had to pay.

■=■

Quicknotes

PETITION FOR CERTIORARI A written request submitted to an appellate court asking that court to hear an appeal from an action in a lower court.

UNCONSCIONABILITY Rule of law whereby a court may excuse performance of a contract, or of a particular contract term, if it determines that such term(s) are unduly oppressive or unfair to one party to the contract.

■=■

Matter of Laurence S. Fordham

State bar (P) v. Attorney (D)

Sup. Jud. Ct. Mass., 423 Mass. 481, 668 N.E.2d 816 (1996),
cert. denied, 519 U.S. 1149 (1997).

NATURE OF CASE: Appeal from a ruling for defendant in case alleging excessive fees were charged by an attorney.

FACT SUMMARY: Fordham (D), an attorney representing a client charged with driving under the influence of alcohol, allegedly charged an excessively high fee.

🏛 **RULE OF LAW**
In determining whether fees are clearly excessive, a court may examine the difficulty of the issues presented, the time and skill required to perform the legal service properly, and the fee customarily charged in the locality for comparable services.

FACTS: The father of an accused drunk driver hired Fordham (D), an experienced litigator in a prestigious Boston law firm, to handle the case, but later refused to pay the fees charged. Bar counsel charged Fordham (D) with charging a clearly excessive fee under DR 2-106(A). Fordham (D) alleged that dishonesty, bad faith or overreaching must be shown for discipline of an attorney. The hearing committee found that Fordham's (D) fee fell within a safe harbor because an agreement existed between a client and an attorney, which protected from challenge the contention that the fee was clearly excessive. Bar counsel (P) appealed to the Supreme Judicial Court.

ISSUE: In determining whether fees are clearly excessive, may a court examine the difficulty of the issues presented, the time and skill required to perform the legal service properly, and the fee customarily charged in the locality for comparable services?

HOLDING AND DECISION: (O'Connor, J.) Yes. In determining whether fees are clearly excessive, a court may examine the difficulty of the issues presented, the time and skill required to perform the legal service properly, and the fee customarily charged in the locality for comparable services. The hearing committee's and the board's determinations that a clearly excessive fee was not charged were not warranted. The amount of time Fordham (D) spent to educate himself and represent his client was excessive despite his good faith and diligence. Disciplinary Rule 2-106 (B)'s mandate, by referring to a lawyer of ordinary prudence, creates explicitly an objective standard by which attorneys' fees are to be judged. Dishonesty, bad faith or overreaching need not be established for discipline to be necessary. A public reprimand is the appropriate sanction for charging a clearly excessive fee. Such a sanction is appropriate in this case. Reversed.

▶ **ANALYSIS**

The court in this case considered eight factors to ascertain the reasonableness of the fee. The first factor required examining the time and labor required, the novelty and difficulty of the questions involved, and the skill requisite to perform the legal service properly. Another factor considered was the fee customarily charged in the locality for similar legal services.

ABA Model Rule 1.5(a) is the modern equivalent to the Mode Code DR2-106(B).

Quicknotes

PUBLIC REPRIMAND An official warning or admonition.

SAFE HARBOR A tax code provision safeguarding the taxpayer from liability in respect to the payment of taxes, so long as he has made an effort to comply with the provisions of the code.

Matter of Cooperman

n/a

N.Y. Ct. App., 83 N.Y.2d 465, 633 N.E.2d 1069 (1994).

NATURE OF CASE: Appeal from temporary suspension from practice following a disciplinary proceeding for professional misconduct.

FACTS SUMMARY: Attorney Cooperman (D) was disciplined for repeatedly using special nonrefundable retainer fee agreements with his clients.

🏛 RULE OF LAW
Special nonrefundable retainer fee agreements are per se violative of public policy.

FACTS: Cooperman (D) charged three separate clients advance minimum fees of $15,000, $5,000, and $10,000 respectively for specific services. All of Cooperman's (D) fee agreements were in writing and stated that the fees were not refundable for any reason, even if the client later decided to discharge him. Shortly after retaining Cooperman (D), all three clients discharged him and demanded refunds. Cooperman (D) refused. The local Grievance Committee (P) warned Cooperman (D) twice not to use nonrefundable retainer fee agreements. The Appellate Division suspended suspended him from practice for two years. Cooperman (D) appealed. He acknowledged that the purpose of the nonrefundable retainer was to prevent clients from firing him but argued that his agreements should not be treated as per se violations because the fees he charged were not clearly excessive.

ISSUE: Are special nonrefundable retainer fee agreements per se violative of public policy?

HOLDING AND DECISION: (Bellacosa, J.) Yes. Special nonrefundable retainer fee agreements are per se violative of public policy. The Code of Professional Responsibility reflects an unqualified right to terminate the attorney-client relationship. If an attorney is discharged before completing their services, he has the right to recover, in quantum meruit, compensation for any services he has actually rendered. Correspondingly, the client should be free to sever the fiduciary relationship with the lawyer. Nonrefundable retainers, however, restrict the client's prerogative to terminate by imposing a penalty—the loss of the entire "nonrefundable" fee, no matter what legal services, if any, were rendered. Moreover, claiming that a particular nonrefundable fee is reasonable does not validate an agreement that impedes a client's absolute right to walk away from his attorney. Cooperman's (D) fee arrangements transgressed professional ethical norms. Affirmed.

▶ ANALYSIS

No other state has chosen to adopt the above prohibition on nonrefundable legal fees. Minimum fee arrangements and general retainers continue to be acceptable in all jurisdictions. Note that some courts may order disgorgement of unethical fees as an additional disciplinary sanction. See, e.g., *United States v. Strawser*, 800 F.2d 704 (7th Cir. 1986).

■══■

Quicknotes

NEW YORK CODE OF PROFESSIONAL RESPONSIBILITY DR 2-106(A) An attorney shall not enter into an agreement for charge, or collect an illegal or excessive fee.

■══■

McQueen, Rains, & Tresch LLP v. CITGO Petroleum Corp.

Law firm (P) v. Client (D)

Okla. Sup. Ct., 195 P.3d 35 (2008).

NATURE OF CASE: Certified questions from federal court to state court in action for liquidated damages under law firm retainer agreement.

FACT SUMMARY: A law firm, McQueen, Rains, & Tresch LLP (MRT) (P), contended that a liquidated damages clause in its engagement agreements with CITGO Petroleum Corp. (D) was enforceable because MRT (P) had altered its position in reliance on the contracts; CITGO (D) was a sophisticated client; the amount of damages was reasonable; the contract terms were unambiguous; and the clause did not constitute a penalty.

🏛 RULE OF LAW
A liquidated damages clause in an engagement agreement between an attorney and a client is enforceable where the clause is unambiguous, the client is sophisticated, the attorney has altered his or her position in reliance on the clause, the amount of damages is reasonable, and the clause does not work a penalty.

FACTS: When CITGO Petroleum Corp.(CITGO) (D), a large corporation, moved it corporate office, three in-house attorneys did not make the move, but instead opened their own law firm, McQueen, Rains, & Tresch LLP (MRT) (P). In a series of agreements, CITGO (D), through its general counsel, negotiated an arrangement with MRT (P) whereby MRT (P) would perform certain legal work for CITGO (D). As part of the arrangement, an engagement agreement, and supplemental engagement agreements, provided for liquidated damages in the event that CITGO (D) terminated MRT (P) without cause. In the agreement, CITGO (D) acknowledged that MRT (P) had undertaken and continued to undertake costs and expenses so it could operate to provide legal services to CITGO (D). The liquidated damages were to be payment by CITGO (D) of monthly installments of a fixed fee due under the agreement. CITGO (D) terminated MRT (P) around halfway through the agreement's four-year term, and MRT (P) sued CITGO (D) in federal court to enforce the liquidated damages provision. The court certified to the state's highest court the question of whether the liquidated damages provision was enforceable, and the state's highest court accepted the certified question.

ISSUE: Is a liquidated damages clause in an engagement agreement between an attorney and a client enforceable where the clause is unambiguous, the client is sophisticated, the attorney has altered his or her position in reliance on the clause, the amount of damages is reasonable, and the clause does not work a penalty?

HOLDING AND DECISION: (Watt, J.) Yes. A liquidated damages clause in an engagement agreement between an attorney and a client is enforceable where the clause is unambiguous, the client is sophisticated, the attorney has altered his or her position in reliance on the clause, the amount of damages is reasonable, and the clause does not work a penalty. First, it should be noted that different jurisdictions are split as to this issue, and in a majority of jurisdictions liquidated damages provisions such as the one presented here are unenforceable as against public policy, unless the attorney can show that he or she has changed position or incurred expenses in reliance on the agreement. Nonetheless, a significant number of jurisdictions uphold such provisions or nonrefundable retainer fees where the fees or damages are reasonable; the contract is negotiated with a sophisticated client and the retainer agreement contains an agreement by the client to compensate the lawyer if the client terminates the relationship; the contract is in writing with a clear statement of the consequences of the provision; or where the attorney, in entering the contract, has changed positions or incurred expenses to meet the needs of the client—as where the attorney must forgo other clients to serve the needs of the contracting client. Here, the unique facts of the case meet the criteria of enforceability. CITGO (D) is a large, sophisticated corporation, and the agreements were negotiated by its general counsel. The terms of the provision are unambiguous, and, at a minimum, MRT (P) changed its position to the extent that it equipped an office and provided legal counsel in an out-of-state location. CITGO (D) acknowledged that MRT (P) altered its position by undertaking costs and expenses to meet CITGO's (D) legal needs. Accordingly, the provision is not per se unenforceable and should be upheld it if is not a penalty. It would not be a penalty if the injury to MRT (P) was difficult or impossible to quantify accurately; if the parties intended to provide for damages rather than a penalty; and amount of the damages was a reasonable pre-breach estimate of the probable loss.

▶ ANALYSIS

In a majority of jurisdictions, liquidated damages provisions are unenforceable, leaving attorneys to recover damages in quantum meruit. In these jurisdictions, the reasoning is that a non-refundable retainer compromises the client's absolute right to terminate the attorney-client relationship. Nevertheless, even in jurisdictions where such contracts are normally

Continued on next page.

struck down as against public policy, an attorney may recover contractual fees if, in entering into such a contract, the attorney has changed positions or incurred expenses.

■━■

Quicknotes

ATTORNEY-CLIENT RELATIONSHIP The confidential relationship established when a lawyer enters into employment with a client.

LIQUIDATED DAMAGES An amount of money specified in a contract representing the damages owed in the event of breach.

PER SE By itself; not requiring additional evidence for proof.

QUANTUM MERUIT Equitable doctrine allowing recovery for labor and materials provided by one party, even though no contract was entered into, in order to avoid unjust enrichment by the benefited party.

RETAINER Fee paid upon employing an attorney in advance of services rendered; sometimes paid to prevent employment by adversary.

■━■

Goldfarb v. Virginia State Bar

Real estate lawyers (P) v. State bar association (D)

421 U.S. 773 (1975).

NATURE OF CASE: Review of order dismissing class action seeking damages and injunctive relief under federal antitrust laws.

FACT SUMMARY: The Goldfarbs (P) contended that a minimum-fee schedule published by the Virginia State Bar (D) constituted price fixing in violation of the Sherman Act.

🏛 RULE OF LAW
Minimum fees mandated by a state bar may constitute price fixing in violation of the Sherman Act.

FACTS: The Goldfarbs (P) sought to engage a lawyer to do a title search on the home they wished to purchase. Per state law, only an attorney could do this. They consulted numerous attorneys, none of whom was willing to do the task for less than the minimum fee published by the Virginia State Bar (D). The Goldfarbs (P) subsequently brought a class action suit, contending that the minimum fee schedule constituted price fixing in violation of the Sherman Antitrust Act. The court of appeals held it was not, and dismissed. The Supreme Court granted review.

ISSUE: May minimum fees mandated by a state bar violate the Sherman Act?

HOLDING AND DECISION: (Burger, C.J.) Yes. Minimum fees mandated by a state bar may constitute price fixing in violation of the Sherman Antitrust Act. To constitute a violation, the minimum fee schedule has to amount to price fixing affecting interstate commerce, and not be subject to an exemption to the Sherman Act. A purely advisory fee schedule would present a different situation, but the record here reveals that attorneys in Virginia are under considerable pressure not to violate the State Bar's (D) fixed, rigid price floor. This being so, the schedule of minimum fees does constitute price fixing. It clearly affects interstate commerce. The Bar (D) argues that an exception should be made for "learned professions." The problem with this argument is that no such exception exists in the Sherman Act. As the Act is expressly designed to reach as broadly as possible, courts should not create exceptions not found in the Act's text. Finally, the Bar (D) argues that the fee schedule does fall within an exception for state action. The record here, however, belies this assertion. The State Bar (D) is not a governmental entity, but a private association to whom some regulatory oversight has been delegated. It is not an arm of either the executive or judicial branches of the state. If the state wanted to directly regulate fees, it could do so. It has not so done, however, so the exception is inapplicable. Therefore, since the fee schedule does constitute price fixing affecting interstate commerce and no exception applies, it violates the Sherman Act. Reversed and remanded.

▶ ANALYSIS

In the 1970s, the Supreme Court began to whittle away at some of the powers that state bars once had to regulate the commercial aspect of lawyer behavior. Fee setting is an example. Another is lawyer advertising. Interestingly, Chief Justice Burger, who wrote the present opinion, was the most vociferous dissenter in the cases that liberalized lawyer advertising.

Quicknotes

MINIMUM FEE SCHEDULES The publication of recommended fee rates to be charged by attorneys; such fee schedules are in violation of federal antitrust laws.

STATE ACTION Actions brought pursuant to the Fourteenth Amendment claiming that the government violated the plaintiff's civil rights.

Evans v. Jeff D.

n/a

475 U.S. 717 (1986).

NATURE OF CASE: Review of invalidation of fee waiver.

FACT SUMMARY: A consent decree ending a civil rights action contained a waiver of statutory attorney fees, a provision invalidated on appeal.

🏛 RULE OF LAW
A consent decree ending a civil rights action may contain a fee waiver.

FACTS: A class of plaintiffs filed a civil rights action against various Idaho officials, contending discrimination against those with certain handicaps. The class was represented by Johnson, a public-interest attorney. Near the time of trial, the state officials made an offer of prospective relief basically giving the plaintiff class all it wanted. The only condition was a waiver of fees awardable under 42 U.S.C. § 1988. The plaintiffs agreed, and a consent decree, including approval of the fee waiver, was entered. Johnson then filed an appeal, contending that such waivers were void as contrary to statute and legal ethics. The Ninth Circuit reversed the approval of the fee waiver, holding it invalid. The state officials petitioned for certiorari.

ISSUE: May a consent decree ending a civil rights action contain a fee waiver?

HOLDING AND DECISION: (Stevens, J.) Yes. A consent decree ending a civil rights action may contain a fee waiver. The text of the Fees Act, codified at 42 U.S.C. § 1988, provides no support for the proposition that Congress intended to ban all fee waivers offered in connection with substantial relief on the merits. The language clearly makes the award of fees discretionary, not mandatory. Further, to hold that waivers are per se invalid would, at least in some cases, run contrary to the intent of the statute, which is promotion of the vindication of civil rights. This is because knowledge that settlement would necessarily involve attorney fees would make settlement less attractive and, therefore, force a trial in some cases where it could have been avoided. Therefore, the better rule is that whether or not a fee waiver will be allowed in any consent decree will be left to the sound discretion of the trial court. [The Court went on to hold that the district court had not abused its discretion in approving the fee waiver.] Reversed.

DISSENT: (Brennan, J.) It is true that neither the language nor the history of § 1988 would tend to preclude fee waivers. It is quite likely that the drafters gave the matter no thought at all. However, the effect of this decision will be to make lawyers more reluctant to take civil rights cases, which is clearly contrary to the intent behind the section. An attorney is ethically bound to accept his client's decision regarding settlement, and knowing that such a decision may end up in noncompensation will certainly not work in favor of an attorney taking a case.

▶ ANALYSIS

The dissent and the majority opinion took entirely different approaches to the issue here. The majority opinion saw this as a straightforward matter of statutory construction. The dissent saw it not only as a statutory issue, but a matter of ethics as well, implicating Ethical Considerations 7-7 and 7-9 of the ABA Model Code of Responsibility.

Quicknotes

CONSENT DECREE A decree issued by a court of equity ratifying an agreement between the parties to a lawsuit; an agreement by a defendant to cease illegal activity.

WAIVER The intentional or voluntary forfeiture of a recognized right.

CHAPTER 5

Concurrent Conflicts of Interest

Quick Reference Rules of Law

Matter of Neville

n\a

Ariz. Sup. Ct., 147 Ariz. 106, 708 P.2d 1297 (1985).

NATURE OF CASE: Appeal from disciplinary action.

FACT SUMMARY: Attorney Neville (D) entered into a real estate transaction with Bly (P), his client, and a third party in which Bly (P) claimed the terms of the contract were adverse to his interest.

🏛 RULE OF LAW

Whenever lawyers knowingly acquire an ownership, possessory, security, or other pecuniary interest adverse to a client, the client must be given a reasonable opportunity to seek the advice of independent counsel.

FACTS: Attorney Neville (D) represented Bly (P), a licensed real estate broker, in certain real estate matters. Neville (D) also purchased options in certain of Bly's (P) properties. Neville (D), Bly (P), and a third party then entered into a contract, drafted by Neville (D), under which one of the Bly (P) properties would go to Neville (D) in exchange for a promissory note. Bly (P) created the substantive terms, and Neville (D) accepted these terms with no negotiation. The Arizona Bar charged Neville (D) with violation of DR 5-104(A), the rule governing attorney-client business deals.

ISSUE: When lawyers knowingly acquire an ownership, possessory, security, or other pecuniary interest adverse to a client, must the client be given a reasonable opportunity to seek the advice of independent counsel?

HOLDING AND DECISION: (Feldman, J.) Yes. Whenever lawyers knowingly acquire an ownership, possessory, security, or other pecuniary interest adverse to a client, the client must be given a reasonable opportunity to seek the advice of independent counsel. In this case, Neville (D) was engaged in a business transaction in which his interests were adverse to those of his client, Bly (P), without giving Bly (P) a reasonable opportunity to seek the advice of independent counsel. DR 5-104 is applicable even in situations in which the attorney did not intend to defraud or act with improper motives. The application of DR 5-104 is not limited to those situations in which the lawyer is acting as counsel in the very transaction in which his interests are adverse to his client. It applies also to transactions in which, although the lawyer is not formally in an attorney-client relationship with the adverse party, it may fairly be said that because of other transactions, an ordinary person would look to the lawyer as a protector rather than as an adversary. Affirmed.

▶ ANALYSIS

The courts are very suspicious of business deals between attorneys and clients, a suspicion that led to the drafting of

Rule 1.8 (a) and DR 5-104 (A). The courts scrutinize such transactions closely despite the fact that lawyers are provided no bright line by which to determine when they can act as ordinary businesspeople in relation to the interests of those whom they have represented in the past or whom they represent on other matters at the present. The courts make it more difficult for lawyers to deal adversely with past and present clients because it is believed that this result conforms to the obligation of the profession and is in the public interest.

■■■

Quicknotes

FIDUCIARY DUTY A legal obligation to act for the benefit of another, including subordinating one's personal interests to that of the other person.

■■■

Gellman v. Hilal

Medical malpractice plaintiff (P) v.

Hospital and two doctors (D)

N.Y. Sup. Ct., 159 Misc. 2d 1085, 607 N.Y.S.2d 853 (1994).

NATURE OF CASE: Defendant's motion for an order disqualifying plaintiff's attorney in a medical malpractice case.

FACT SUMMARY: Because Hilal (D) had previously been represented by the wife of Gellman's (P) present attorney, Bogaty, Hilal (D) sought to disqualify Bogaty as a conflicted lawyer.

🏛 RULE OF LAW
Lawyers who are related as parent, child, sibling, or spouse may represent direct adversaries only if the clients consent after consultation.

FACTS: Gellman (P) sued Hilal (D) for medical malpractice. Gellman (P) was represented by Bogaty, whose wife, Brody, had previously represented Hilal (D) in another malpractice action whose subject was the same medical procedure challenged by Gellman (P). Hilal (D) therefore moved to disqualify Bogaty in the current action. Hilal (D) argued that if Brody divulged her knowledge to Bogaty, Hilal (D) would be prejudiced. Hilal (D) also argued that, as Bogaty's wife, Brody had a financial incentive to aid Bogaty in the prosecution of Gellman's (P) suit since any contingent fee he earned would likely benefit the Brody-Bogaty marital household; Hilal (D) also alleged a danger of inadvertent disclosure in the ordinary course of spousal intimacy of daily life in a shared household.

ISSUE: May lawyers who are related as parent, child, sibling or spouse represent direct adversaries if the clients consent after consultation?

HOLDING AND DECISION: (Sklar, J.) Yes. Lawyers who are related as parent, child, sibling, or spouse may represent direct adversaries only if the clients consent after consultation. In the context of attorney-spouses working for opposing law firms, there is no per se rule of disqualification based on marital status. A lawyer is not automatically disqualified from a case because he or she is related or has a personal relationship with the opposing counsel. Here, Hilal (D), who relied solely on the hearsay, vague, and conclusory affidavits of his counsel, has not alleged facts sufficient for the court to infer that Bogaty is privy to confidences or other strategic information that if revealed might injure Hilal (D) in the instant action or that, even if she had such knowledge, she has or will improperly divulge it to Hilal's (D) detriment. Motion denied.

▶ ANALYSIS

Generally, the danger of inadvertent revelation of confidences among spouses and relatives is not fatal as long as attorney-spouses adhere carefully to ethical guidelines set forth in the Canons, Ethical Considerations, and the Disciplinary Rules. However, despite the permissiveness of some states regarding possible attorney-spouse conflicts of interest, there are other states that insist on limits. Michigan, for one, extends the imputation of conflict to cohabitating lawyers, and California requires the disclosure of any intimate personal relationship with the opponent's attorney.

■■■

Quicknotes

NEW YORK RULES OF PROFESSIONAL RESPONSIBILITY 9 101(D) A lawyer related to another lawyer as parent, child, sibling or spouse shall not represent in any matter a client whose interests differ from those of another party to the matter who the lawyer knows is represented by the other lawyer unless the client consents to the representation after full disclosure and the lawyer concludes that the lawyer can adequately represent the interests of the client.

■■■

Cuyler v. Sullivan

Unidentified (P) v. Convicted murderer (D)

446 U.S. 335 (1980).

NATURE OF CASE: Review of habeas corpus granted subsequent to murder conviction.

FACT SUMMARY: Sullivan (D), convicted of murder, was granted habeas corpus because the court found the possibility of conflict in his representation.

🏛 RULE OF LAW
The mere potential of a conflict of interest in representation is not sufficient to invalidate a conviction.

FACTS: Sullivan (D) was accused of murder, along with two accomplices. Sullivan (D) was tried separately, his trial occurring first. He was represented by two attorneys, who also represented the accomplices. His attorneys rested without presenting evidence. Sullivan (D) was convicted. He appealed, contending that a conflict of interest existed as to his representation. The conviction was affirmed. He petitioned for habeas corpus. At a hearing, one attorney testified that the decision not to present a case was due to a weak state case. The other testified that he didn't wish to reveal the testimony of certain witnesses, in view of the upcoming trial of the accomplices. The district court denied habeas corpus, but the court of appeals reversed, holding that since a possibility of conflict existed, Sullivan (D) had been denied effective counsel. The Supreme Court granted review.

ISSUE: Is the mere potential of a conflict of interest in representation sufficient to invalidate a conviction?

HOLDING AND DECISION: (Powell, J.) No. The mere potential of a conflict of interest in representation is not sufficient to invalidate a conviction. The potential for a conflict of interest exists in every situation involving multiple representation, so to hold that the mere potential of a conflict is sufficient to invalidate a conviction would end multiple representation. However, in many cases multiple representation actually improves the position of the defendant. In light of this, this Court believes that only an actual conflict, as opposed to a potential conflict, should invalidate a conviction. Prejudice is presumed when a conflict exists, but should not be when one is only possible. Reversed and remanded.

CONCURRENCE: (Brennan, J.) A court should undertake its own inquiry as to whether a conflict exists.

CONCURRENCE AND DISSENT: (Marshall, J.) The trial court has a duty to ascertain that multiple representation is the product of the defendant's informed choice.

▶ ANALYSIS

No objection was made by Sullivan (D) to multiple representation in the underlying trial. In his habeas corpus petition, Sullivan (D) contended that a court should undertake its own investigation to determine the potential for conflicts. Justices Brennan and Marshall took exception to the Court's ruling in this regard.

Quicknotes

CONFLICT OF INTEREST Refers to ethical problems that arise, or may be anticipated to arise, between an attorney and his client if the interests of the attorney, another client or a third party conflict with those of the present client.

HABEAS CORPUS A proceeding in which a defendant brings a writ to compel a judicial determination of whether he is lawfully being held in custody.

Wheat v. United States

Drug conspirator (D) v. U.S. (P)

486 U.S. 153 (1988).

NATURE OF CASE: Appeal from conviction for federal narcotics laws violations.

FACT SUMMARY: Ruling that a conflict existed, the district court refused to allow Wheat (D) to retain the same counsel who was representing Wheat's (D) codefendants.

⎯ RULE OF LAW
If a trial court believes that representation of a defendant by an attorney presents a serious potential for conflict, the court may refuse to permit that representation, even in the face of a waiver.

FACTS: Wheat (D) was indicted, along with Gomez (D) and Bravo (D), for violation of federal narcotics laws. Shortly before his trial, Wheat (D) requested that the court allow him to substitute in as counsel of record Iredale, who also represented Gomez (D) and Bravo (D), who had pleaded guilty but whose plea bargains had not as yet been accepted. The government (P) objected, contending that if the court elected not to permit Gomez's (D) and Bravo's (D) plea bargains, Wheat (D) would almost certainly be called as witness at their subsequent trials. This would, said the government (P), put Iredale in conflict among his clients. Wheat (D) offered a waiver. Nonetheless, the court, finding strong probability of conflict, refused to allow Iredale to substitute in. Wheat (D) was convicted, and he appealed, contending he had been denied the right to counsel per the Sixth Amendment. The court of appeals affirmed, and the Supreme Court granted review.

ISSUE: If a trial court believes that representation of a defendant by an attorney presents a serious potential for conflict, may the court refuse to permit the representation, even in the face of a waiver?

HOLDING AND DECISION: (Rehnquist, C.J.) Yes. If a trial court believes that representation of a defendant by an attorney presents a serious potential for conflict, the court may refuse to permit that representation, even in the face of a waiver. The Sixth Amendment guarantees the right to effective counsel, not the right to counsel of choice. The guiding purpose behind the Amendment is to ensure a fair trial. While this goal has been interpreted to create a presumption in favor of permitting a party to retain counsel of choice, if the exercise of such choice leads to the potential for a fair trial to be unlikely, this presumption must give way. The possibility of waiver does not alter this conclusion. Courts have an interest in being sustained on appeal, and appellate courts can and do find waivers invalid in ineffective-assistance-of-counsel claims. The decision of whether to permit a representation that poses a threat of conflict is best made by the trial court, and nothing in the record here shows that the district court violated the standards articulated above. Affirmed.

DISSENT: (Marshall, J.) The propriety of the district court's order thus depends on whether the government (P) showed that the particular facts and circumstances of the multiple representation proposed in this case were such as to overcome the presumption in favor of a defendant's choice of counsel. It appears they were not.

DISSENT: (Stevens, J.) The Court gives insufficient weight to the informed and voluntary nature of Wheat's (D) waiver.

▶ ANALYSIS

The Supreme Court has never held that the Sixth Amendment guarantees the right to counsel, but it is not absolute. It appears that the only certain right a defendant has regarding choice of representation is the right to waive counsel and represent himself, if he so chooses. This right was announced in *Faretta v. California*, 422 U.S. 806 (1975).

■=■

Quicknotes

CONFLICT OF INTEREST Refers to ethical problems that arise, or may be anticipated to arise, between an attorney and his client if the interests of the attorney, another client or a third party conflict with those of the present client.

SUBSTITUTION OF COUNSEL Refers to a situation in which a party seeks to terminate representation by a particular attorney or an attorney seeks to withdraw from a case; in order to substitute attorneys the party or attorney must obtain the court's permission, which may be denied if such substitution would result in an unfair delay or disruption of the proceedings.

■=■

Young v. United States ex rel. Vuitton et Fils S.A.

Infringer of trademark (D) v. Manufacturer of leather goods (P)

481 U.S. 787 (1987).

NATURE OF CASE: Review of criminal contempt citation.

FACT SUMMARY: In a criminal contempt proceeding ancillary to a trademark infringement suit, counsel for Vuitton (P) was appointed as prosecutor against Young (D).

🏛 RULE OF LAW
Counsel for a party that is a beneficiary of a court order may not be appointed as a prosecutor in a contempt action alleging a violation of order.

FACTS: Vuitton et Fils. S.A. (Vuitton) (P) filed a trademark infringement action against, among others, Young (D). Vuitton (P) obtained an injunction. After Young (D) violated the injunction, Vuitton (P) brought an action to show cause why Young (D) should not be held in contempt. Counsel for Vuitton (P) was appointed prosecutor. Young (D) was convicted, and the court of appeals confirmed.

ISSUE: May counsel for a party that is the beneficiary of a court order be appointed as prosecutor in a contempt action alleging violation of that order?

HOLDING AND DECISION: (Brennan, J.) No. Counsel for a party that is the beneficiary of a court order may not be appointed as prosecutor in a contempt action alleging a violation of that order. The role of the criminal prosecutor is not to convict, but to seek justice. For that reason, prosecutors are forbidden by both federal law and professional ethics from representing the government in which they, their family, or their business associates have an interest. This Court has consistently applied to criminal contempt proceedings the same standards applicable to criminal prosecutions in general, and believes this prohibition to be applicable to such proceedings. Therefore, a prosecutor in a criminal contempt matter cannot have an interest in the order upon which the contempt is based. Here, counsel for Vuitton (P), the beneficiary of the allegedly violated order, was appointed prosecutor. Vuitton (P) plainly had an interest in seeing the order enforced. Counsel was therefore placed in a position of serving two masters, justice and Vuitton (P). This was improper and mandates a new trial. Reversed.

▌ANALYSIS

The role of the prosecutor is described in various places in the law. A notable example is EC 7-13 of the ABA Model Code of Professional Responsibility. Per this section, prosecutors are ethically bound not to prosecute unless they are convinced of guilt.

■=■

Quicknotes

18 U.S.C. § 208(A) Federal prosecutors are prohibited from representing the government in any matter in which they, their family, or their business associates have any interest.

■=■

Fiandaca v. Cunningham

Female prison inmates (P) v. State (D)

827 F.2d 825 (1st Cir. 1987).

NATURE OF CASE: Appeal of injunction issued in action based on alleged equal protection violation.

FACT SUMMARY: A settlement offer made by the State of New Hampshire (D) to a class of plaintiffs was contrary to the interest of another client of the offeree's attorney.

🏛 RULE OF LAW
An attorney may not represent two clients when a settlement offer made to one is contrary to the interests of the other.

FACTS: A class of plaintiffs comprised of female inmates of the New Hampshire (D) penitentiary system brought action in which they claimed that they were denied equal protection because male inmates enjoyed superior facilities. They were represented by New Hampshire Legal Assistance (NHLA), a public-interest legal organization. NHLA also represented a class of students at a state school in an unrelated matter. At one point the State (D) offered to convert one of the school buildings into a penitentiary for women. The students represented by NHLA vehemently opposed this, and the convict plaintiffs rejected the offer. A trial ensued, and the district court held that the State (D) penitentiary system denied equal protection to female convicts and ordered that a facility be built. The State (D) appealed, contending that the court should have disqualified NHLA from representing the plaintiff class.

ISSUE: May an attorney represent two clients when a settlement offer made to one is contrary to the interest of the other?

HOLDING AND DECISION: (Coffin, J.) No. An attorney may not represent two clients when a settlement offer made to one is contrary to the interests of the other. Rule 1.7 of New Hampshire's Rules of Professional Conduct prohibits an attorney from representing a client if the representation of that client may be materially limited by the lawyer's responsibilities to another client. Loyalty to a client is materially limited when a lawyer cannot recommend a possible course of action due to loyalty to another client. Thus, when a settlement offer is made and a lawyer owes allegiance to a party opposed to that settlement, that lawyer cannot use his independent judgment in advising the client. At this point a conflict exists. Here, NHLA could not recommend the State's (D) settlement offer because of a duty to another client, and it therefore should have been disqualified. [The court went on to affirm the finding of an equal protection violation, holding it not to have been tainted by the conflict, but ordered a retrial as to the remedy.] Vacated and remanded for a new trial.

▶ ANALYSIS

It is usually possible for a potential conflict to be waived. This requires (1) a reasonable belief by the attorney that he can zealously represent both interests, and (2) a knowing consent by the affected parties. The court here, however, believed the conflict to be real, not potential.

Quicknotes

CLASS ACTION A suit commenced by a representative on behalf of an ascertainable group that is too large to appear in court, who shares a commonality of interests and who will benefit from a successful result.

CONFLICT OF INTEREST Refers to ethical problems that arise, or may be anticipated to arise, between an attorney and his client if the interests of the attorney, another client or a third party conflict with those of the present client.

NEW HAMPSHIRE RULES OF PROFESSIONAL CONDUCT 1.7 Prohibits an attorney from representing a client if such representation may be materially limited by the lawyer's responsibilities to another client.

Simpson v. James

Restaurant owner (P) v. Attorney (D)

903 F.2d 372 (5th Cir. 1990).

NATURE OF CASE: Appeal of award of damages for professional malpractice.

FACT SUMMARY: Simpson (P), who retained Oliver (D) to represent her legally during the sale of her business, alleged that Oliver (D) committed malpractice by representing the buyers of her business as well.

> ## 🏛 RULE OF LAW
> An attorney may commit malpractice by representing both sides in a transaction.

FACTS: Simpson (P) operated a restaurant, which she desired to sell. She contacted James (D), an attorney who had previously represented her, concerning a sale. Oliver (D), James' (D) partner, facilitated a transaction between Simpson (P) and Tide Creek, Inc. A deal was arranged wherein the business was sold for $500,000, $100,000 of which was paid down, with $400,000 payable in notes, secured by Tide Creek stock. The business proved unprofitable for Tide Creek, which eventually went bankrupt. Simpson (P) sued Oliver (D) and James (D), who had represented both sides in the transaction, contending that it had constituted malpractice for them to do so. A jury awarded Simpson (P) $200,000, and an appeal was taken.

ISSUE: May an attorney commit malpractice by representing both sides in a transaction?

HOLDING AND DECISION: (Wisdom, J.) Yes. An attorney may commit malpractice by representing both sides in a transaction. While representing both sides is not inherently impermissible, it may make it difficult for an attorney to represent one side, the other, or both as zealously as professional standards require. Here, the jury found that James' (D) and Oliver's (D) failure to adequately safeguard Simpson's (P) pecuniary interests, such as creating a lien on Tide Creek's stock rather than the business' assets, proximately harmed Simpson (P). This was a permissible finding for the jury. Affirmed.

▌ ANALYSIS

Upon examination, it can be concluded that dual representation didn't really figure into the result here, at least not directly. The malpractice was not a conflict of interest, although the conflict might have caused the behavior that constituted the malpractice. It would seem that an attorney who didn't represent the buyers would have been equally liable had he acted as did the defendants here. The facts given in the opinion do not shed light on whether the attorney would have acted differently absent the dual representation, so it is impossible to say whether the dual representation led to the malpractice.

◼━◼

Quicknotes

CONFLICT OF INTEREST Refers to ethical problems that arise, or may be anticipated to arise, between an attorney and his client if the interests of the attorney, another client or a third party conflict with those of the present client.

NEGLIGENCE Conduct falling below the standard of care that a reasonable person would demonstrate under similar conditions.

◼━◼

Public Service Mutual Insurance Co. v. Goldfarb

Insurance company (P) v. Dentist (D)

N.Y. Ct. App., 53 N.Y.2d 392, 425 N.E.2d 810, 442 N.Y.S.2d 422 (1981).

NATURE OF CASE: Action for declaratory judgment of insurance noncoverage.

FACT SUMMARY: Public Service Mutual Insurance Co. (P) contended that Goldfarb's (D) acts of sexual assault on a dental patient did not trigger a duty to defend and indemnify him in a civil suit.

🏛 RULE OF LAW
Sexual assault by a doctor against a patient may trigger a professional liability carrier's duty to defend and indemnify in a subsequent civil suit.

FACTS: Goldfarb (D), a dentist, was accused by one of his patients of sexually assaulting her while she was under sedation. Criminal charges were filed, and he was convicted. The victim filed a civil suit against Goldfarb (D), which he tendered to his professional liability carrier, Public Service Mutual Insurance Co. (P). Public Service (P) responded by seeking a declaration that the alleged acts did not trigger a duty to defend and indemnify Goldfarb (D). [The casebook excerpt does not state the trial court or appellate division results.]

ISSUE: May sexual assault by a doctor against a patient trigger a duty to defend and indemnify in a subsequent civil suit?

HOLDING AND DECISION: (Jasen, J.) Yes. Sexual assault by a doctor against a patient may trigger a professional liability carrier's duty to defend and indemnify in a subsequent civil suit. To the extent that a jury in the civil suit finds that injury upon the victim was unintentionally caused, the duty to indemnify will arise. Since this determination cannot be made prior to trial, Public Service (P) must defend Goldfarb (D) for as long as the potential of a duty to indemnify exists, the duty to defend also exists. [The casebook excerpt does not state whether the present opinion constituted a reversal, affirmation, or modification.]

▶ ANALYSIS

The reasoning used in arriving at the rule here is fairly universal. The duty to defend arises when any aspect of an action might be covered. The terminology used is "the duty to defend is broader than the duty to indemnify." The most influential case in this area is *Gray v. Zurich Ins. Co.*, 65 Cal. 2d 263 (1966), the first case to clearly delineate the broadness of the duty to defend.

Quicknotes

COMPENSATORY DAMAGES Measure of damages necessary to compensate victim for actual injuries suffered.

INDEMNIFICATION The payment by a corporation of expenses incurred by its officers or directors as a result of litigation involving the corporation.

PUNITIVE DAMAGES Damages exceeding the actual injury suffered for the purposes of punishment, deterrence and comfort to plaintiff.

■━■

CHAPTER **6**

Successive Conflicts of Interest

Quick Reference Rules of Law

Analytica, Inc. v. NPD Research, Inc.

Competing company (P) v. Research company (D)

708 F.2d 1263 (7th Cir. 1983).

NATURE OF CASE: Appeal of order disqualifying counsel.

FACT SUMMARY: The same law firm that once represented NPD Research, Inc. (D) represented a former principal of NPD in a subsequent suit against it.

🏛 RULE OF LAW
A law firm may not represent a principal of a former client in a lawsuit against the former client.

FACTS: Malec was an employee of NPD Research, Inc. (NPD) (D), who was given an equity interest as compensation for certain services. The law firm of Schwartz & Freeman handled the transaction. Subsequent to this, Malec left NPD (D), forming Analytica, Inc. (P), which established itself as a competitor of NPD in market research. Analytica (P) subsequently filed an antitrust action against NPD (D). Analytica (P) was represented by Schwartz & Freeman. NPD (D) moved to disqualify Schwartz & Freeman. The district court granted the motion, and Analytica (P) appealed.

ISSUE: May a law firm represent a principal of its former client in a lawsuit against the former client?

HOLDING AND DECISION: (Posner, J.) No. A law firm may represent a principal of its former client in a lawsuit against the former client. Specifically, a lawyer may not represent an adversary of his former client if the subject matter of the two representations is substantially related. If confidential information that might have been obtained during a representation might be relevant in the second, then the attorney must be disqualified. The fact that the attorney might not have actually attained the information is of no consequence. A per se rule of disqualification is preferable, as determination of the facts underlying a motion to disqualify would be difficult and time consuming if a case-by-case analysis were employed. Here, Schwartz & Freeman represented NFID (D) in a financial transaction, and then represented an adversary in an antitrust suit. It seems clear that information that the firm might have obtained during its representation of NPD (D) might be relevant in the present action, so disqualification was proper. Affirmed.

▶ ANALYSIS

The rule stated here is universal. In the current age of megafirms, it sometimes presents a problem in that disqualification of one member of a firm usually disqualifies the entire firm. A large firm might have many clients and the possibilities of inadvertent conflicts are ever present.

Quicknotes

CONFLICT OF INTEREST Refers to ethical problems that arise, or may be anticipated to arise, between an attorney and his client if the interests of the attorney, another client or a third party conflict with those of the present client.

■=■

Cromley v. Board of Education

Teacher (P) v. School (D)

17 F.3d 1059 (7th Cir.), *cert. denied*, 513 U.S. 816 (1994).

NATURE OF CASE: Appeal from judgment granting defendant's motion for summary judgment and denying plaintiff's motion to disqualify defendants' attorneys in § 1983 action.

FACT SUMMARY: During Cromley's (P) suit against the Board of Education (D), her attorney, Weiner, withdrew from the case after accepting a partnership in the law firm representing the Board (D), but the district court denied Cromley's (P) motion to disqualify the Board's (D) attorneys.

🏛 RULE OF LAW
When a lawyer in a case moves to the other party's law firm, the attorneys for the other party must be disqualified where the representations are substantially related, unless the presumption of shared confidences can be rebutted.

FACTS: Cromley (P), a high school teacher, brought an action under 42 U.S.C. § 1983 against the Board of Education (the Board) (D), claiming she had been denied various administrative positions because she had complained to a state agency about the sexual misconduct of a co-worker. During extended pretrial litigation, Cromley's (P) attorney, Weiner, accepted a partnership in the law firm representing the Board (D). Weiner then withdrew as Cromley's (P) attorney. The district court granted summary judgment to the Board (D), denying Cromley's (P) motion to disqualify the Board's (D) attorneys. Cromley (P) appealed.

ISSUE: When a lawyer in a case moves to the other party's law firm, must the attorneys for the other party be disqualified where the representations are substantially related, unless the presumption of shared confidences can be rebutted?

HOLDING AND DECISION: (Ripple, J.) Yes. When a lawyer in a case moves to the other party's law firm, the attorneys for the other party must be disqualified where the representations are substantially related, unless the presumption of shared confidences can be rebutted by the establishment of a screening process. The subject matter both before and after Weiner changed law firms was Cromley's (P) lawsuit against the Board (D). However, in this case, the presumption of shared confidences has been successfully rebutted by the timely establishment of a screening process. After he joined the Board's (D) law firm, Weiner was denied access to the relevant files. Under threat of discipline, he and all employees of the firm were admonished not to discuss the case. In addition, Weiner was not allowed to share in the fees derived from the case. The partner handling the case for the Board (D) affirmed under oath that all of the admonitions have been adhered to. Affirmed.

▶ ANALYSIS

Other factors help to determine whether adequate protection of the former client's confidences has been achieved. Those factors include the size of the law firm, its structural divisions, the screened attorney's position in the firm, the likelihood of contact between the screened attorney and one representing another party, and the fact that a law firm's and lawyer's most valuable asset are their reputations for honesty, integrity, and competence. The presumption of shared confidences has been found to be irrebuttable only when an entire law firm changes sides.

■≡■

Quicknotes

CONFLICT OF INTEREST Refers to ethical problems that arise, or may be anticipated to arise, between an attorney and his client if the interests of the attorney, another client or a third party conflict with those of the present client.

■≡■

Armstrong v. McAlpin

Receiver (P) v. Alleged theives (D)

625 F.2d 433 (2d Cir. 1980) (en banc), *vacated on other grounds*, 449 U.S. 1106 (1981).

NATURE OF CASE: Appeal of denial of motion to disqualify attorney of record.

FACT SUMMARY: Altman, an attorney who had been involved in an Securities and Exchange Commission (SEC) investigation against McAlpin (D), later joined the firm representing the receiver appointed to recover allegedly stolen funds, which McAlpin (D) contended constituted a conflict.

🏛 RULE OF LAW
It is not a per se ground for disqualification when an attorney involved in a government investigation joins a private firm involved in litigation concerning the same matter.

FACTS: The Securities and Exchange Commission (SEC) commenced an investigation against McAlpin (D) and others, believing them to have looted the company they controlled. A receiver was eventually appointed to attempt to recover the company's funds. The firm of Gordon Hurwitz was retained by Armstrong (P), the receiver. Altman, who had been an attorney with the SEC and was involved in the original probe, was now a new attorney at Gordon Hurwitz. McAlpin (D) moved to disqualify Gordon Hurwitz, contending that the presence of Altman constituted a conflict. The district court, after receiving testimony that Altman was screened from ongoing litigation, denied the motion. A Second Circuit panel reversed, holding that government service per se disqualifies a firm which included a former government attorney from handling an action in which the attorney had previously been involved. The Second Circuit held a rehearing en banc.

ISSUE: Is it a per se ground for disqualification when an attorney involved in a government investigation joins a private firm involved in litigation concerning the same matter?

HOLDING AND DECISION: (Feinberg, J.) No. It is not a per se ground for disqualification when an attorney involved in a government investigation joins a private firm involved in litigation concerning the same matter. Under DR 5-105(D) of the ABA Code of Professional Responsibility, the disqualification of one firm member disqualifies the entire firm. However, policy reasons exist for not applying this rule when the cause of the conflict is prior government service. If it were applied, it would be extremely difficult for the government to obtain qualified lawyers to work for it, as they would face the prospect of being unable to obtain private employment ever again. Rather, the better review is to consider disqualification on a case-by-case basis. If a court finds the prior government attorney to be effectively screened from the private litigation,

disqualification is not necessary. Here, that was the holding of the district court, and it was a proper ruling. Panel opinion vacated; district court affirmed. [On a petition for certiorari, the Supreme Court held the order nonappealable, and vacated both the panel and the en banc options.]

▶ ANALYSIS

Due to the proliferation of both government and large, multi-state law firms, the problem addressed here has become more common in recent years. The solution reached by the district court, accepting a screening of the disqualified attorney from the litigation in question, has been the most common response. While technically a violation of DR 5-105(D), this "Chinese wall" approach has been accepted in many jurisdictions.

■━■

Quicknotes

DISQUALIFICATION A determination of unfitness or ineligibility.

■━■

CHAPTER 7

Ethics in Advocacy

Quick Reference Rules of Law

Nix v. Whiteside

Unidentified (P) v. Convicted killer (D)

475 U.S. 157 (1986).

NATURE OF CASE: Review of order granting habeas corpus subsequent to murder conviction.

FACT SUMMARY: Whiteside (D) contended that his counsel's refusal to allow him to commit perjury denied him his right to counsel.

🏛 RULE OF LAW
A criminal defendant is not denied his right to counsel if his counsel refuses to allow him to commit perjury.

FACTS: An altercation involving Whiteside (D) resulted in the stabbing death of another. Prior to testifying, Whiteside (D) told his attorney that he intended to state that he had seen a gun in the decedent's hand, even though he had previously stated to the contrary. The attorney informed him that to do so would constitute perjury, which he could not allow. The attorney informed Whiteside (D) that if he did so testify, he would inform the court of Whiteside's (D) perjury. Whiteside (D) did not so testify, and he was convicted of murder. He appealed, contending that counsel's threats to expose his perjury constituted a denial of counsel under the Sixth Amendment. This conviction was affirmed. Whiteside (D) petitioned for habeas corpus in district court. This was denied. The court of appeals reversed, agreeing with Whiteside's (D) contention. The Supreme Court granted review.

ISSUE: Is a criminal defendant denied his right to counsel if his counsel refuses to allow him to commit perjury?

HOLDING AND DECISION: (Burger, C.J.) No. A criminal defendant is not denied his right to counsel if his counsel refuses to allow him to commit perjury. The Sixth Amendment's right to counsel clause is not abridged unless counsel is so ineffective as to not have been functioning as counsel. It is the duty of the counsel to take all lawful measures to exonerate his client. However, counsel has no right to violate the law, or to assist others in doing so. Further, DR 7-102 of the ABA Code of Professional Responsibility prohibits an attorney from knowingly using perjured testimony or false evidence. Since counsel is not permitted to assist in perjury, it can hardly be considered ineffectiveness when he refuses to do so. Here, the only basis for Whiteside's (D) contention regarding ineffectiveness was the refusal to allow him to perjure himself, and therefore no Sixth Amendment violation occurred. Reversed.

CONCURRENCE: (Blackmun, J.) Whiteside's (D) argument is that he would have been acquitted had he been allowed to testify falsely. The answer to this is that the prevention of perjury can never be the basis for a conclusion that the trial was unfair, and therefore a defendant can never claim prejudice due to such prevention.

CONCURRENCE: (Stevens, J.) It should be remembered that recollections can and do augment themselves upon reflection, and the question is open as to how counsel should behave if it is not clear, as it was here, that perjury was in the offing.

▶ ANALYSIS

It has never been affirmatively held that an accused has an absolute right to testify on his own behalf. In fact, at one time an accused was categorically prohibited from such testimony. While not expressly approving such a right, the Court here simply noted in passing that such a right is universally recognized.

■━■

Quicknotes

PERJURY The making of false statements under oath.

■━■

Mullaney v. Aude

Ex-boyfriend (D) v. Ex-girlfriend (P)

Md. Ct. Spec. App., 126 Md. App. 639, 730 A.2d 759 (1999).

NATURE OF CASE: Appeal from imposition of attorneys' fees.

FACT SUMMARY: Mullaney's (D) lawyer, Mr. Harris, insulted both Ms. Aude (P) and Ms. Green, her attorney, by making gender-biased remarks and insinuations during a deposition in front of other attorneys.

🏛 RULE OF LAW
A lawyer may not use gender-biased tactics to gain advantage during the course of the litigation process.

FACTS: One of the defendant's lawyers, Mr. Harris, made a derogatory comment to the plaintiff during the course of a deposition. When Ms. Green, one of the plaintiff's lawyers, told Mr. Harris that his remark was in poor taste and asked him to refrain from making any further derogatory statements, Mr. Harris insulted Ms. Green by making nasty insinuations and further referring to Ms. Green as "babe."

ISSUE: May a court properly impose attorneys' fees as a sanction for using gender bias in the litigation process to gain an advantage over an adversary?

HOLDING AND DECISION: (Adkins, J.) Yes. Courts have a duty to require the attorneys who practice before them to conduct themselves in a professional manner. That includes refraining from behavior and statements that are biased or prejudiced based on race, sex, religion, national origin, disability, age, sexual orientation, or socioeconomic status. The court makes clear that the use of gender-bias tactics to evoke an emotional reaction in an adversary will not be tolerated. Affirmed.

▶ ANALYSIS

This case is one of many clearly calling for a return to civility. Judges do not indulge this and other types of less blatant behavior and often impose sanctions and other forms of discipline. Foul language and name calling are other forms of intimidation that are not permitted.

■══■

Quicknotes

DEPOSITION A pretrial discovery procedure whereby oral or written questions are asked by one party of the opposing party or of a witness for the opposing party under oath in preparation for litigation.

■══■

Matter of Thonert

n\a

733 N.E.2d 932 (Ind. 2000).

NATURE OF CASE: Appeal from a finding of misconduct.

FACT SUMMARY: A lawyer failed to reveal to the court legal authority that was directly adverse to his client's position.

🏛 RULE OF LAW
An attorney has an affirmative duty to disclose adverse legal authority within the controlling jurisdiction to the court when the opposing party fails to do so and the attorney is aware of the law.

FACTS: The respondent, a lawyer, represented a client in an appeal and raised a case in support of his argument on behalf of his client. The same lawyer had over one year earlier argued another case, *Fletcher*, that addressed similar issues but the ruling in which was directly opposite to the premise the lawyer was currently setting forth. The lawyer failed to reveal to the court the adverse case law in which he himself had previously been involved and about which he clearly knew.

ISSUE: May a court sanction a lawyer for failing to reveal adverse legal authority to a tribunal when the attorney knows about the conflicting law and the opposing party fails to reveal it?

HOLDING AND DECISION: (Per curiam) Yes. Attorneys have a duty to reveal to a court legal authority in the controlling jurisdiction that the lawyer knows is directly contrary to his or her client's position and that is not disclosed by the opposing side. The premise behind this requirement is that the judge should have all of the legal information available to properly reach a sound decision, thereby creating good law. Affirmed.

▶ ANALYSIS

The sanction selected to impose on this attorney was a public reprimand. In the grand scheme of the offenses lawyers can commit while practicing their profession and the array of sanctions judges can impose, the punishment here seems to squarely fit the crime. The court also ruled that a lawyer must inform his or her client of adverse precedent.

■▬■

Quicknotes

AFFIRMATIVE DUTY An obligation to undertake an affirmative action for the benefit of another.

DUTY TO DISCLOSE The duty owed by a fiduciary to reveal those facts that have a material effect on the interests of the party that must be informed.

■▬■

Special Issues in Litigation

Quick Reference Rules of Law

In re Ryder

n\a

263 F. Supp. 360 (E.D. Va. 1967).

NATURE OF CASE: Court's own motion to suspend attorney from practice for criminal misconduct.

FACTS SUMMARY: Ryder, an attorney, hid stolen money and a sawed-off shotgun belonging to his client in a safe-deposit box at his bank, intending to keep it there until after his client's trial for armed robbery.

🏛 **RULE OF LAW**
A defense attorney's withholding of incriminating evidence during a criminal proceeding for the purpose of hindering the preparation of the prosecution's case constitutes unethical deception and misconduct.

FACTS: Cook robbed a bank at gunpoint and deposited the proceeds as well as his sawed-off shotgun in a bank safe-deposit box. Some of the cash Cook obtained was "bait money," the serial numbers of which had been recorded. During an interview with the FBI, Cook turned over some of this "bait money," but called Ryder, an attorney who had represented him in a previous civil matter, and asked him to attend the interview. Ryder did and had the agents leave. Cook then insisted he had not robbed the bank and had obtained the money at a crap game. Ryder telephoned one of the FBI agents, who told him that the serial numbers of the money Cook turned over matched some of those taken from the bank. Ryder then again asked Cook about the robbery, but Cook replied that on the day of the robbery a man had offered him $500 to put a package in a safe-deposit box. Ryder then consulted with various attorneys and judges in confidence about whether it would be proper to have a third party obtain the money in Cook's box and what would constitute a proper course of conduct thereafter. The advice of these lawyers was mixed and ambiguous. Ryder then asked Cook to execute a power of attorney authorizing access to Cook's safe-deposit box and authorizing him to dispose of its contents "as he saw fit" and "in a way that wouldn't harm Cook." Cook did so. Ryder then went to the bank and transferred the contents of Cook's box, the stolen money and the sawed-off shotgun, to a box in his own name. Ryder did not intend to notify the prosecution about this evidence, but only intended to turn it over if the government learned of it independently. Cook was then indicted for armed robbery, and FBI agents with search warrants for both Cook's and Ryder's boxes found Cook's contraband and weapon. The local federal district court then removed Ryder as Cook's counsel, suspended him from practice, referred the matter to the local U.S. Attorney, and set a hearing for further disciplinary proceedings against Ryder.

ISSUE: Does a defense attorney's withholding of incriminating evidence during a criminal proceeding for the purpose of hindering the preparation of the prosecutor's case constitute unethical deception and misconduct?

HOLDING AND DECISION: (Per curiam) Yes. A defense attorney's withholding of incriminating evidence during a criminal proceeding for the purpose of hindering the preparation of the prosecutor's case constitutes unethical deception and misconduct. Ryder took possession of the stolen money and sawed-off shotgun specifically to destroy the chain of evidence linking his client to the robbery. He intended to retain the evidence until at least after Cook's trial, unless the government first discovered it and compelled its production. Ryder knew that the money was stolen, that the man who robbed the bank used a sawed-off shotgun, that Cook's possession of the shotgun was illegal, and that his larceny was a continuing offense. He also knew that the laws against concealing stolen property and forbidding receipt and possession of a sawed-off shotgun contained no exemptions for lawyers such as himself. Thus, Ryder used the office of attorney in violation of the law in an effort to destroy an evidentiary presumption. Ryder would be disbarred were it not for two factors in mitigation: he intended to return the money after Cook's trial; and he consulted several attorneys before deciding on a course of conduct he may have believed constituted acting in the best interests of his client. [Ryder was ordered suspended from the practice of law for 18 months.] Affirmed.

▶ **ANALYSIS**

The holdings of other cases are in accord with this decision. See, e.g., *People v. Superior Court (Fairbank)*, 192 Cal. App. 3d 32, 237 Cal. Rptr. 158 (1987) (a criminal defense lawyer must inform the court that he has taken possession of stolen property at issue in the criminal proceeding, even if it cannot be shown that the prosecution "needs" the evidence to prepare its case). See also *Commonwealth v. Stenbach*, 356 Pa. Super. 5, 514 A.2d 114 (1986), leave to appeal denied 517 Pa. 589, 534 A.2d 769 (1987) (lawyers are under an ethical obligation to turn over physical evidence to opposing counsel or to the court). Cf. N.Y. State Bar Committee on Professional Ethics, Opinion No. 479 (Mar. 6, 1978) (attorney whose client was indicted for murder learned from the client the location of the bodies of victims of prior murders and actually took photographs of the bodies; it was held that it was not improper for the attorney

Continued on next page.

to fail to reveal the location of the bodies or to use this knowledge with his client's approval in plea bargaining).

■══■

Quicknotes

ATTORNEY-CLIENT PRIVILEGE A doctrine precluding the admission into evidence of confidential communications between an attorney and his client made in the course of obtaining professional assistance.

POWER OF ATTORNEY A written instrument which allows a person to appoint an agent and confer authority to perform certain specified acts on his behalf.

■══■

People v. Meredith

State (P) v. Convicted robber and murderer (D)

Cal. Sup. Ct., 29 Cal. 3d 682, 631 P.2d 46, 175 Cal. Rprt. 612 (1981).

NATURE OF CASE: Appeal of conviction of robbery and murder.

FACT SUMMARY: An investigator working for criminal defendant Scott's (D) attorney observed and took possession of a wallet that had been taken from the victim and disposed of by Scott (D).

 RULE OF LAW
The attorney-client privilege does not protect from disclosure testimony regarding observations made by counsel or his agent concerning evidence which has been removed by counsel or the agent.

FACTS: Meredith (D) was charged with the robbery and murder of one Wade. Also charged was Scott (D). Scott (D) told Schenk, his counsel, that after Meredith (D) had killed Wade, Scott (D) took Wade's wallet and disposed of it in a trash container near Scott's (D) home. Schenk dispatched Frick, an investigator, to retrieve the wallet. Frick found the wallet and brought it to Schenk, who eventually turned it over to the prosecution. At trial, Frick was subpoenaed to testify about where he had found the wallet. The testimony was admitted over Scott's (D) attorney-client privilege objection. Scott (D) was convicted, and the state court of appeals affirmed. The California Supreme Court granted review.

ISSUE: Does the attorney-client privilege protect from disclosure testimony regarding observations made by counsel or his agent concerning evidence which has been removed by counsel or agent?

HOLDING AND DECISION: (Tobriner, J.) No. The attorney-client privilege does not protect from disclosure testimony regarding observations made by counsel or his agent concerning evidence which has been removed by counsel or the agent. Deciding this issue requires the balancing of competing considerations. On the one hand, to deny protection to observations arising from confidential communications could chill protected attorney-client communication. On the other hand, the privilege cannot be extended so far as to render immune from discovery evidence first obtained by the defense. It cannot be doubted that communications between counsel and his investigator are protected by the privilege. From this it is not a large step to conclude that information acquired solely as a result of such communications are also protected. Here, Frick's knowledge of the location of the wallet was a result of information obtained from Schenk, so, without more, introduction of testimony regarding his observations would be protected. However, when counsel or his agent takes the extra step of moving or altering the evidence, the opportunity

of the prosecution to observe it is forever lost. To hold that testimony regarding the original state of the evidence cannot be compelled under these circumstances would effectively permit the defense to destroy critical evidence, a result not contemplated by the attorney-client privilege. Here, Frick did in fact remove the wallet, so the prosecution was properly permitted to question him concerning it. Affirmed.

ANALYSIS

Both the law and the Code of Professional Responsibility place a duty on attorney with respect to evidence. As to testimonial evidence, an attorney may not facilitate perjury. As to tangible evidence, an attorney may not falsify the same. The subject is covered in Disciplinary Rule 7-102(A).

Quicknotes

ATTORNEY-CLIENT PRIVILEGE A doctrine precluding the admission into evidence of confidential communications between an attorney and his client made in the course of obtaining professional assistance.

DUTY OF CANDOR / DUTY OF FAIRNESS The ethical duty to turn over an instrumentality of crime once it has been used to aid a client's case, owed to the tribunal and opposing counsel to prevent the frustration of justice.

Zubulake v. UBS Warburg LLC

Employee (P) v. Employer (D)

229 F.R.D. 422 (S.D.N.Y. 2004).

NATURE OF CASE: Discovery and sanction motions in discrimination action.

FACT SUMMARY: [Facts not stated in casebook excerpt.]

🏛 RULE OF LAW
When a party reasonably anticipates litigation, or litigation has commenced, and the party has a duty to put in place a "litigation hold" to ensure the preservation of relevant information, counsel has: a duty to oversee and monitor compliance with the litigation hold; a duty to ensure that all sources of potentially relevant information are identified and placed "on hold"; and an ongoing duty to ensure the preservation of the information so identified.

FACTS: [Facts not stated in casebook excerpt.]

ISSUE: When a party reasonably anticipates litigation, or litigation has commenced, and the party has a duty to put in place a "litigation hold" to ensure the preservation of relevant information, does counsel have: a duty to oversee and monitor compliance with the litigation hold; a duty to ensure that all sources of potentially relevant information are identified and placed "on hold;" and an ongoing duty to ensure the preservation of the information so identified?

HOLDING AND DECISION: (Schiendlin, J.) Yes. When a party reasonably anticipates litigation, or litigation has commenced, and the party has a duty to put in place a "litigation hold" to ensure the preservation of relevant information, counsel has: a duty to oversee and monitor compliance with the litigation hold; a duty to ensure that all sources of potentially relevant information are identified and placed "on hold;" and an ongoing duty to ensure the preservation of the information so identified. Once a party reasonably anticipates litigation, it must suspend its routine document retention/destruction policy and put in place a "litigation hold" to ensure the preservation of relevant documents. As a general rule, that litigation hold does not apply to inaccessible backup tapes made for disaster recovery purposes. This duty requires counsel to communicate on an ongoing basis to ensure that the litigation hold is implemented and that all sources of potentially relevant information are identified, that the relevant information is retained, and that, unless privileged, is produced to the opposing party. To fulfill his or her duties, counsel must become fully familiar with the client's document retention policies and client's data retention architecture. This invariably involves speaking with the client's information technology personnel. It also involves communicating with all "key players" in the litigation to understand how each one of them stores potentially relevant information. For example, had this been done in this case, some relevant information would have been discovered and produced two years before it actually was produced. Where a company is too large for counsel to speak with every relevant employee, it may be possible to run a system-wide keyword search, with counsel preserving a copy of each "hit." Counsel does not have to review each "hit," but merely has to ensure that the "hits" are retained. When the opposing party propounds its document requests, the parties could negotiate a list of search terms to be used in identifying responsive documents, and counsel would only be obliged to review documents that came up as "hits" on the second, more restrictive search. As this demonstrates, counsel must take reasonable affirmative steps to monitor compliance with the litigation hold so that all sources of discoverable information are identified and searched. Next, once the party and counsel have identified all the sources of potentially relevant information, they must retain that information, and produce it upon request to the opposing party. Rule 26 imposes a duty to supplement responsive discovery requests when the party or its counsel discover that a prior response was incorrect, and from this it can be inferred that there is a duty to ensure that discoverable information is not lost. While the duty is nominally the party's, in practice it falls on counsel. Thus, there is a continuing duty to ensure that the relevant information is preserved. To meet the burden of this duty, counsel not only must issue a "litigation hold" but must periodically reissue it so that new employees are aware of it, and so that it is fresh in the minds of all employees. Counsel must also clearly communicate the contours of the litigation hold with all the "key players," and must periodically remind them of their ongoing preservation duty. Finally, counsel should instruct all employees to produce electronic copies of their relevant active files, and must also make sure that all backup media which the party is required to retain are identified and stored safely. To achieve this, counsel must typically communicate with the client's information technology personnel and must explain to them the necessity of segregating relevant backup tapes from others so that the possibility that such tapes will be inadvertently recycled is eliminated.

▶ ANALYSIS

The rules and guidelines enunciated by Judge Schiendlin in the five *Zubulake* opinions—which are considered groundbreaking precedent in the United States on e-discovery—are applicable to both in-house counsel as well as outside counsel. For in-house counsel, this means being very

Continued on next page.

familiar with the company's document retention policies and data storage and retrieval infrastructure. Law firms serving as outside counsel must obtain such knowledge for every client, which is more cumbersome. In either case, counsel must, to some extent, become an expert in e-discovery and understand how data is created, stored and retrieved electronically.

■━■

Quicknotes

DISCOVERY Pretrial procedure during which one party makes certain information available to the other.

■━■

Jovanovic v. City of New York

Falsely convicted individual (P) v. Municipality (D)

2006 U.S. Dist. LEXIS 59165 (S.D.N.Y. 2006).

NATURE OF CASE: Motion to dismiss in action under 42 U.S.C. § 1983 for, inter alia, denial of a fair trial due to prejudicial publicity by the prosecution.

FACT SUMMARY: Jovanovic (P), who had been falsely accused and convicted of kidnapping, sexual abuse, and assault, contended that Fairstein (D), the prosecutor in the case, had made such highly inflammatory and prejudicial extrajudicial statements to the press following his arraignment and throughout his criminial proceedings that she effectively denied him the right to a fair trial. He also claimed that the City of New York (City) (D) was separately liable for Fairstein's (D) actions because it had a widespread custom of permitting prosecutors to make inflammatory and prejudicial statements to the press in high-profile criminal cases. Fairstein (D) defended by moving to dismiss, claiming that Jovanovic (P) had failed to adequately plead his claim, and that, in any event, Fairstein (D) was protected from suit by the doctrines of absolute and qualified immunity. The City (D) asserted that the claim against it failed as a matter of law.

🏛 RULE OF LAW
(1) A claim for denial of a fair trial due to prejudicial publicity by the prosecution will not be dismissed where a plaintiff falsely convicted of a crime has expressly alleged that the prosecution made improper statements and leaks during the pre-trial proceedings and that the plaintiff was in fact denied a fair trial, but has not expressly claimed that other pre-trial remedies were of no avail to remedy the prejudicial effect of the leaks or statements.

(2) A prosecutor does not have absolute immunity for extrajudicial statements she has made to the press that are beyond the scope of her official duties as a prosecutor.

(3) A prosecutor does not have qualified immunity for making a continuing stream of extrajudicial statements to the press where a reasonable prosecutor would know that such conduct would result in denial of a fair trial to the accused.

(4) A claim of municipality liability for prosecutorial misconduct will not be dismissed where the plaintiff has alleged with some specificity that the municipality has a widespread and permanent custom of permitting prosecutors to make prejudicial extrajudicial statements to the press in high-profile cases.

FACTS: Ruzcek, a college student, reported to Bonilla (D), a police officer for the City of New York (City) (D), that she had been severely sexually assaulted by Jovanovic (P), a doctoral candidate, for 20 hours. Ruzcek and Jovanovic (P) had corresponded by email prior to the alleged incident. The physical evidence did not at all match Ruzcek's assertions of hogtying, violent rape, sodomy, burning, gagging, and assault with a club. In addition, her accounts of the alleged assault kept changing and were contradictory. She waited four days before seeking medical treatment, "despite her claims that she experienced profuse bleeding, severe burns and intense pain." Moreover, she had a history of making false sexual accusations, and in fact, had falsely accused her own father and uncle of sexual molestation, and, a week before filing her own complaint against Jovanovic (P), she had encouraged an acquaintance to file a false rape complaint. Despite the seriousness of Ruzcek's allegations, Bonilla (D) waited nine days before attempting to question Jovanovic (P). When Jovanovic (P) requested an attorney, Bonilla (D) arrested him on charges of rape, sodomy, and unlawful imprisonment. No evidence was found in his apartment that corroborated Ruzcek's allegations. Bonilla (D), however, fabricated false and misleading police reports regarding the evidence and Jovanovic's (P) arrest, and repeated these falsities to a grand jury. Jovanovic (P) was then arraigned. Following the arraignment, Fairstein (D), the prosecutor, made highly inflammatory and prejudicial remarks about Jovanovic (P) to the press. These included statements such as: "He terrorized this young woman to the point that she was too frightened to call the authorities until weeks after it happened"; "He tied her to a chair, undressed her, and tortured her with sex toys and other objects for almost a full day"; "[H]e tortured and sexually abused the woman, burning her with candle wax, biting her, sexually assaulting her and threatening to dismember her as Jeffrey Dahmer, the serial killer, had done with his victims"; He "tied the woman's legs to a chair and gagged her before sexually torturing her"; "[H]e was so prepared for this and carried it off so smoothly"; "We believe this was not the first time he did something like this"; and "We believe there are other victims." These statements made the headlines of every local newspaper, and the case quickly became known as the first internet-related sex prosecution. Throughout the proceedings, Fairstein (D) continued to provide highly damaging leaks to the press, including select portions of the email correspondence between Ruzcek and Jovanovic (P) that served to demonize Jovanovic (P). Trial witnesses were influenced by the media coverage and their testimony was tainted by it. A jury convicted Jovanovic (P) of kidnapping, sexual abuse, and assault, and he was sentenced to a term of 15 years to life in prison. He served more than 20 months in

Continued on next page.

prison, where he was repeatedly strip-searched, and threatened and attacked (once almost resulting in his death) by other inmates. The state's intermediate appellate court then reversed Jovanovic's (P) conviction, finding that the trial judge had improperly hampered his defense. Anticipating a second trial, the prosecution offered several plea deals over a period of close to two years, but Jovanovic (P) maintained his innocence and refused the deals. The prosecution finally moved to dismiss all charges against Jovanovic (P), which were dismissed with prejudice. Thereafter, Jovanovic (P) brought suit in federal district court under 42 U.S.C. § 1983 against Fairstein (D) and the City (D) for, inter alia, denial of a fair trial due to prejudicial publicity by the prosecution [Bonilla (D) was also a defendant on other claims]. Jovanovic (P) claimed that Fairstein (D) had made such highly inflammatory and prejudicial extrajudicial statements to the press following his arraignment and throughout his criminial proceedings that she effectively denied him the right to a fair trial. He also claimed that the City (D) was separately liable for Fairstein's (D) actions because it had a widespread custom of permitting prosecutors to make inflammatory and prejudicial statements to the press in high-profile criminal cases. Fairstein (D) defended by moving to dismiss, claiming that Jovanovic (P) had failed to adequately plead his claim, and that, in any event, Fairstein (D) was protected from suit by the doctrines of absolute and qualified immunity. The City (D) asserted that the claim against it failed as a matter of law. [A separate statute of limitations defense was rejected by the court.]

ISSUE:

(1) Will a claim for denial of a fair trial due to prejudicial publicity by the prosecution be dismissed where a plaintiff falsely convicted of a crime has expressly alleged that the prosecution made improper statements and leaks during the pre-trial proceedings and that the plaintiff was in fact denied a fair trial, but has not expressly claimed that other pre-trial remedies were of no avail to remedy the prejudicial effect of the leaks or statements?

(2) Does a prosecutor have absolute immunity for extrajudicial statements she has made to the press that are beyond the scope of her official duties as a prosecutor?

(3) Does a prosecutor have qualified immunity for making a continuing stream of extrajudicial statements to the press where a reasonable prosecutor would know that such conduct would result in denial of a fair trial to the accused?

(4) Will a claim of municipality liability for prosecutorial misconduct be dismissed where the plaintiff has alleged with some specificity that the municipality has a widespread and permanent custom of permitting prosecutors to make prejudicial extrajudicial statements to the press in high-profile cases?

HOLDING AND DECISION: (Crotty, J.)

(1) No. A claim for denial of a fair trial due to prejudicial publicity by the prosecution will not be dismissed where a plaintiff falsely convicted of a crime has expressly alleged that the prosecution made improper statements and leaks during the pre-trial proceedings and that the plaintiff was in fact denied a fair trial, but has not expressly claimed that other pre-trial remedies were of no avail to remedy the prejudicial effect of the leaks or statements. To prevail upon a claim for denial of a fair trial due to prejudicial publicity, a plaintiff must establish three elements: (1) that there were improper leaks; (2) that the plaintiff had in fact been denied a fair trial; and (3) that other remedies (e.g., voir dire, peremptory challenges, and challenges for cause) were not available, or were used to no avail, to alleviate the effects of the leaks. Here, Fairstein (D) and the City (D) argue that the claim must be dismissed because Jovanovic (P) failed to plead the third element. They rely on a case where the falsely convicted plaintiff also failed to plead this element. However, their reliance on this case is misplaced because that case teaches that by pleading the first two elements, the plaintiff withstands a motion to dismiss and that particularity in pleading the third element is not necessary at the pleading stage. Thus, the case actually suggests that Fairstein's (D) and the City's (D) motion to dismiss should be denied—not granted. Reliance by them on another case is also misguided. In that case, the court determined that voir dire and peremptory challenges purged the jury of the prejudicial effects of the prejudicial prosecutorial conduct, and the plaintiff had been acquitted, thereby creating the strong presumption that the jury was unbiased. Thus, that case is distinguishable from Jovanovic's (P) case, since he was convicted, suggesting that Fairstein's (D) continuous leaks eliminated the pre-trial procedural safeguards. Jovanovic (P) still has a heavy burden of proving his case at trial, but at this point in the proceedings, taking his allegations as true, there remains the possibility that he will be able to prove his claims. Therefore, the claim against Fairstein (D) will not be dismissed.

(2) No. A prosecutor does not have absolute immunity for extrajudicial statements she has made to the press that are beyond the scope of her official duties as a prosecutor. A prosecutor has absolute immunity for statements made within the scope of her prosecutorial duties. If at all, only qualified good faith immunity attaches to extraneous statements made by a prosecutor that are designed to gain an unfair advantage at trial. Here, Fairstein's (D) statements to the press outside the courtroom can reasonably be described as beyond the scope of her official prosecutorial duties. Therefore, she does not have absolute immunity from Jovanovic's (P) denial of fair trial claim.

(3) No. A prosecutor does not have qualified immunity for making a continuing stream of extrajudicial statements to the press where a reasonable prosecutor would know that such conduct would result in denial of a fair trial to the accused. At the time Fairstein (D) made her continued stream of prejudicial statements to the press, she

Continued on next page.

knew that an accused had a constitutional right to a fair trial, free from the taint of prejudice occasioned by extrajudicial statements to the press such as she had made. A reasonable prosecutor would have known that Jovanovic's (P) constitutional right to a fair trial might be violated by making a continuing stream of prejudicial extrajudicial statements. Here, Fairstein (D) has shown that she fully understood the damaging effects of pretrial publicity. Accordingly, to the extent that Jovanovic (P) can prove that Fairstein (D) actually committed the acts she is accused of, she is not entitled to qualified immunity for those acts.

(4) No. A claim of municipality liability for prosecutorial misconduct will not be dismissed where the plaintiff has alleged with some specificity that the municipality has a widespread and permanent custom of permitting prosecutors to make prejudicial extrajudicial statements to the press in high-profile cases. A municipality may be sued under § 1983 as a "person," but may not be held liable for the actions of its employees on a theory of respondeat superior. Municipalities may be held liable only for their own misdeeds, as where the municipality's customs or policies result in constitutional deprivation. Thus, here, Jovanovic (P) must plead a City (D) custom or policy that led to his being deprived of a fair trial. Jovanovic (P) has pled that the City (D) had a widespread and permanent custom (not an official policy) of permitting prosecutors to make prejudicial extrajudicial statements to the press in high-profile cases. He has adduced evidence of such conduct in other high profile cases, involving named prosecutors as well as police officials. He has also alleged a deliberate indifference by the City (D) to the training and supervision of prosecutors, which was so widespread and severe that it led to a "practice" of prosecuting innocent citizens for crimes they did not commit. At this point in the pleadings, these allegations are sufficient, if proved, to establish municipal liability. Therefore, even though Jovanovic's (P) allegations are vague, they are sufficient to withstand a motion for judgment on the pleadings.

▶ ANALYSIS

Fairstein (D), who left the New York City's District Attorney's office in 2002, and who has continued to consult, write, lecture and serve as a sex crimes expert for a wide variety of print and television media outlets—as well as being an internationally selling author of sex crime novels—herself has commented that the period in which prosecutorial statements—as well as those by the defense—have the greatest impact is during pretrial, since the jury pool is saturated with the information made by the prosecution to the media. She has said that: The period of greatest impact is pretrial because that could be anywhere from three months to a year. Depending on the coverage, people can become immersed in reading about the case. And from this

reading-and-listening public come the people who sit on our juries. After the trial has begun, the jurors are given a rule—that they don't read or listen to media accounts of the case. Most people try hard to comply. But it's almost impossible with the highest-profile cases for it to really happen. When a case like Chambers, the jogger, the subway bomber or the World Trade Center bomber is on trial in New York—and it is literally a page A1 headline—our jurors are coming to work on the subway and the bus . . . mean you can't sit on a train and not see what's there . . . . And you deal with a jury pool that is just saturated with that kind of information. You hope that you get jurors who are telling you the truth, that they can set aside what they've heard and just listen to the evidence in the courtroom. In the end, both sides use the press to great advantage before you get anywhere near the trial stage. The court took these statements into account when determining that Fairstein (D) should not be entitled to qualified immunity because she knew the impact her continued statements could have in denying Jovanovic (P) a fair trial.

■■■■■

Quicknotes

BURDEN OF PROOF The duty of a party to introduce evidence to support a fact that is in dispute in an action.

DISMISSAL WITH PREJUDICE A final determination of an action without a trial on the merits and prohibiting the parties to bring the same action at a later date.

INTER ALIA Among other things.

MOTION TO DISMISS Motion to terminate an action based on the adequacy of the pleadings, improper service or venue, etc.

PEREMPTORY CHALLENGE Challenge brought by a party to a lawsuit of a prospective juror without the need to specify a particular reason.

QUALIFIED IMMUNITY An affirmative defense relieving officials from civil liability for the performance of activities within their discretion so long as such conduct is not in violation of an individual's rights pursuant to law as determined by a reasonable person standard.

VOIR DIRE Examination of potential jurors on a case.

■■■■■

Negotiation and Transactional Matters

Quick Reference Rules of Law

Fire Insurance Exchange v. Bell

Insurance company (D) v. Injured claimant (P)

Ind. Sup. Ct., 643 N.E.2d 310 (1994).

NATURE OF CASE: Appeal from denial of motion for summary judgment.

FACT SUMMARY: Jason Bell (P), a claimant against Fire Insurance Exchange (D), an insurance company, argued that his attorney had the right to rely on the insurance company attorney's intentional misrepresentations as to the company's policy limits.

🏛 RULE OF LAW
An attorney has the right to rely upon representations made by opposing counsel.

FACTS: Jason Bell (P), an infant, was severely burned by leaking gasoline at his grandfather's apartment. His guardian sued the insurer of the apartment. Robert Collins was retained to represent Bell (P) in his insurance claims. During negotiations, counsel for the insurance company intentionally made misrepresentations to Collins as to the limits of insurance coverage, stating the limits to be $100,000 when actually the limits were $300,000. Collins subsequently informed Bell (P) he had intentionally been deceived by the opposing insurance counsel, whereupon Bell (P) brought suit against Fire Insurance Exchange (D), the insurer, for its attorneys' fraudulent misrepresentation of the policy limits. Fire Insurance Exchange (D) moved for summary judgment, arguing there was no right to rely on its attorneys' representations. The motion was denied, and Fire Insurance Exchange (D) appealed.

ISSUE: Does an attorney have the right to rely upon representations made by opposing counsel?

HOLDING AND DECISION: (Dickson, J.) Yes. An attorney has the right to rely upon representations made by opposing counsel. Courts have a particular constitutional responsibility with respect to the supervision of the practice of law. The reliability and trustworthiness of attorney representations constitute an important component of the efficient administration of justice. A lawyer's representations have long been accorded a particular expectation of honesty and trustworthiness. In this regard, the Indiana Oath of Attorneys includes the promise that a lawyer will employ such means only as are consistent with truth. Furthermore, the Indiana Professional Responsibility Rules declare that it is professional misconduct for a lawyer to engage in conduct involving dishonesty, fraud, deceit, or misrepresentation. Numerous other sources of guidelines and standards for lawyer conduct emphasize this basic principle. This court, accordingly, rejects the argument that plaintiff's counsel had no right to rely on the representations he claims because he had the means to ascertain the relevant facts, was sophisticated, was in an adverse position, and that accurate policy limits information could have been obtained through formal discovery. This court declines to require attorneys to burden unnecessarily the courts and litigation process with discovery to verify the truthfulness of material representations made by opposing counsel. The law should promote lawyers' care in making statements that are accurate and trustworthy and should foster the reliance upon such statements by others. Affirmed.

▶ ANALYSIS

As emphasized in the *Bell* decision, in fulfilling the duty to represent a client vigorously, lawyers need be mindful of their obligation to the administration of justice, which is a truth-seeking process designed to resolve human and societal problems in a rational, peaceful, and efficient manner.

■═■

Quicknotes

ATTORNEY-CLIENT PRIVILEGE A doctrine precluding the admission into evidence of confidential communications between an attorney and his client made in the course of obtaining professional assistance.

■═■

Hoyt Properties, Inc. v. Production Resources Group, L.L.C.

Landlord (P) v. Tenant (D)

Minn. Sup. Ct., 736 N.W.2d 313 (2007).

NATURE OF CASE: Appeal from reversal of a summary judgment dismissal of an action to invalidate a settlement agreement.

FACT SUMMARY: Production Research Group, L.L.C. (PRG) (D) contended that a statement made by its attorney to Hoyt Properties (Hoyt) (P) that there was no basis for piercing the corporate veil of its subsidiary, Entolo, to reach PRG (D) was not a fraudulent misrepresentation of fact but a legal opinion, and that, therefore, a release agreement reached between Hoyt (P) and PRG (D) should not be rescinded on the basis of PRG's (D) attorney's statement to Hoyt (P).

🏛 RULE OF LAW

(1) A statement made by an attorney is actionable as a fraudulent misrepresentation where it is a statement implying the existence of facts that support a legal opinion.
(2) A statement by an attorney is actionable as a fraudulent misrepresentation where it constitutes a direct factual assertion.
(3) A genuine issue of material fact is created by an attorney's statements that are actionable as fraudulent misrepresentations where there is a genuine issue of material fact as to whether the attorney either knew his statements were false when made or did not know whether they were true or false.

FACTS: Hoyt Properties (Hoyt) (P) brought an eviction action against Production Research Group, L.L.C. (PRG) (D) and its subsidiary, Entolo. Hoyt (P) settled with Entolo and entered into release discussions with PRG (D), but before agreeing to release PRG (D) from liability, Hoyt's (P) owner had a conversation with PRG's (D) attorney. Hoyt's (P) owner said, "I don't know of any reason how we could pierce the [corporate] veil, do you?" Hoyt (P) alleged that that PRG's (D) attorney responded, "There isn't anything. PRG and Entolo are totally separate." Hoyt (P) claimed that, relying on the statement made by PRG's (D) attorney, it agreed to release PRG (D). Subsequently, Hoyt (P) learned that a complaint in another action alleged contradictory facts that would support piercing the corporate veil. Hoyt (P) brought suit to rescind the release, claiming that PRG's (D) attorney's response had been a fraudulent misrepresentation. To succeed, Hoyt (P) would have to prove that the attorney's statement had been knowingly false and that Hoyt (P) had relied on it. The trial court dismissed the action on summary judgment, but the state's

intermediate appellate court reversed. The state's highest court granted review.

ISSUE:

(1) Is a statement made by an attorney actionable as a fraudulent misrepresentation where it is a statement implying the existence of facts that support a legal opinion?
(2) Is a statement by an attorney actionable as a fraudulent misrepresentation where it constitutes a direct factual assertion?
(3) Is a genuine issue of material fact created by an attorney's statements that are actionable as fraudulent misrepresentations where there is a genuine issue of material fact as to whether the attorney either knew his statements were false when made or did not know whether they were true or false?

HOLDING AND DECISION: (Page, J.)

(1) Yes. A statement made by an attorney is actionable as a fraudulent misrepresentation where it is a statement implying the existence of facts that support a legal opinion. PRG (D) argues that both parts of the attorney's response were legal opinions made in response to a question relating to a legal claim. PRG (D) contends that the use of the word "separate" in the attorney's second sentence is a legal term of art that "does not describe a particular factual predicate in a piercing-the-veil case, but rather, a general legal conclusion that piercing is not warranted." In contrast, Hoyt (P) asserted that the representation that "There isn't anything" implied that the attorney believed there was nothing about PRG's (D) and Entolo's business operations to justify a piercing claim. Hoyt (P) also asserted that the representation that "PRG and Entolo are totally separate" was a direct factual statement bolstering the prior assertion that there were no facts supporting a veil-piercing claim. Under the summary judgment standard, the representations at issue must be viewed in the light most favorable to Hoyt (P). In such a light, the attorney's first sentence was a representation that no facts existed that would support a piercing claim. Even if that sentence was a legal opinion, it nevertheless implied that the attorney was aware of no facts supporting such a claim. Since the statement was not an expression of a pure legal opinion, but a statement implying the existence of facts supporting a legal opinion, the attorney's representation in the first sentence was actionable. Affirmed as to this issue.

Continued on next page.

(2) Yes. A statement by an attorney is actionable as a fraudulent misrepresentation where it constitutes a direct factual assertion. The representation made by the attorney's second sentence, when viewed in the light most favorable to Hoyt (P) under the summary judgment standard, is a direct factual assertion that relationship between PRG (D) and Entolo was such that there were no facts to support a piercing claim. Accordingly, this representation is actionable. Affirmed as to this issue.

(3) Yes. A genuine issue of material fact is created by an attorney's statements that are actionable as fraudulent misrepresentations where there is a genuine issue of material fact as to whether the attorney either knew his statements were false when made or did not know whether they were true or false. For the attorney's statements to be fraudulent they must have been made with the attorney's knowledge of their falsity when made or made without knowing whether they were true or false. Here, whether the attorney knew his representations were false when made requires an assessment of the parties' credibility and weighing the evidence. These tasks cannot be done on summary judgment. Absent evidence in the record establishing, as a matter of law, that the representations were not knowingly false when made, there is a genuine issue of material fact for trial on that issue. There is also a genuine issue of material fact as to whether the attorney made the representations without knowing whether they were true or false. He knew about the complaint brought in the separate, third party action, which alleged facts that would support a piercing claim. However, he had not formed an opinion, one way or the other, about those alleged facts. This could lead a trier of fact to conclude that when the attorney made the representations, he did not know whether they were true. Affirmed as to this issue.

ANALYSIS

Justice Anderson dissented, finding that because the first element of a claim for fraudulent misrepresentation is only met if the false factual representation by the party involves a "fact susceptible of knowledge," PRG's (D) attorney's representations could not be actionable. Justice Anderson reasoned that in order for the attorney to imply facts that "[t]here isn't anything" to a veil-piercing claim, the attorney would have to imply a factual assertion that the second prong of the piercing claim is met, i.e., that the claim is "necessary to avoid injustice or fundamental unfairness." Because this is a subjective inquiry made by a court, it is not a "fact susceptible of knowledge," and even if it was, it would be unreasonable to conclude that the attorney falsely implied that a veil-piercing claim would not meet this prong. In other words, if PRG's (D) attorney was to evaluate the claim and decide that it was viable, the attorney would have to conclude that it would be unjust and fundamentally unfair for the attorney's client to escape liability. Those are not the type of conclusions an attorney

is expected to make, and they are generally not susceptible of the attorney's knowledge. Similarly, because the two-prong test for piercing the corporate veil is a subjective test applied by the court, the attorney could not be in a position to know (1) what facts any particular court or factfinder might find significant, and (2) which factors under the first prong the court might apply, since the enumerated factors in case law are not exhaustive. Therefore, Justice Anderson found it difficult to see how the attorney could as a matter of law represent that "no facts" existed to support a piercing claim, given that a court could find a fact significant that no other court ever had in the past.

Quicknotes

CORPORATE VEIL Refers to the shielding from personal liability of a corporation's officers, directors or shareholders for unlawful conduct engaged in by the corporation.

ISSUE OF MATERIAL FACT A fact that is disputed between two or more parties to litigation that is essential to proving an element of the cause of action or a defense asserted, or which would otherwise affect the outcome of the proceeding.

SETTLEMENT AGREEMENT An agreement entered into by the parties to a civil lawsuit agreeing upon the determination of rights and issues between them, thus disposing of the need for judicial determination.

SUMMARY JUDGMENT Judgment rendered by a court in response to a motion made by one of the parties, claiming that the lack of a question of material fact in respect to an issue warrants disposition of the issue without consideration by the jury.

Virzi v. Grand Trunk Warehouse and Cold Storage Co.

Injured party (P) v. Company (D)

571 F. Supp. 507 (E.D. Mich. 1983).

NATURE OF CASE: Motion to set aside settlement in personal injury action.

FACT SUMMARY: Counsel for Virzi (P) obtained a settlement in his behalf, soon thereafter learned of his death, and failed to reveal same to opposing counsel and the court at a confirmation hearing.

🏛 RULE OF LAW
Counsel for a deceased party must inform counsel and the court of his client's demise if such death is relevant to the litigation.

FACTS: Virzi (P) sued Grand Trunk Warehouse and Cold Storage Co. (D) for personal injuries. A mediation was held. Unbeknownst to all involved, Virzi (P) had died of causes unrelated to the case several days prior to the mediation. The mediator valued the case at $35,000. Grand Trunk (D), on counsel's advice, accepted the figure. A hearing to confirm the settlement was held. Prior to the hearing, Virzi's (P) counsel became aware of Virzi's (P) death. He did not reveal this fact at the hearing because he was not so asked. The district court confirmed the settlement. Grand Trunk's (D) counsel learned of Virzi's (P) death and moved to set aside the settlement.

ISSUE: Must counsel for a deceased party inform counsel and the court of his client's demise if such death is relevant to the litigation?

HOLDING AND DECISION: (Gilmore, J.) Yes. Counsel for a deceased party must inform counsel and the court of his client's demise if such death is relevant to the litigation. While an attorney is under a clear duty not to make false assertions of fact to the court and opposing counsel, an attorney's duty of candor is higher than that. This candor involves a requirement of disclosing information essential to the merits of a suit, whether asked about the relevant facts or not. In this instance, whether or not Virzi (P) was alive was certainly a matter that went to the very essence of the value of the case, and counsel's failure to reveal Virzi's (P) demise constituted a sharp practice that cannot be condoned. Motion granted.

▌ANALYSIS

It is universally accepted that an attorney is under a duty to reveal adverse legal authority to a court. The obligation to reveal adverse facts is less clear. Lying to courts is, of course, prohibited, but the jurisdictions vary about the extent to which adverse information must be volunteered.

Quicknotes

ATTORNEY-CLIENT PRIVILEGE A doctrine precluding the admission into evidence of confidential communications between an attorney and his client made in the course of obtaining professional assistance.

■═■

The Florida Bar v. Belleville

State bar (P) v. Attorney (D)

Fla. Sup. Ct., 591 So. 2d 170 (1991).

NATURE OF CASE: Appeal from decision of state bar referee.

FACT SUMMARY: Walter Belleville (D), an attorney for one party, induced an unrepresented adverse party to sign legal documents which the unrepresented adverse party did not understand. Belleville (D) was charged with violation of ethical duties.

🏛 RULE OF LAW
An attorney has a duty to explain to an unrepresented opposing party the fact that the attorney is representing an adverse interest and must explain the material terms of the documents involved.

FACTS: Walter Belleville (D), a Florida attorney, was retained as counsel for Bradley Bloch to negotiate an agreement with James Cowan to purchase property owned by the latter. Cowan was eighty-three years of age and had a third-grade education. The various written agreements overwhelmingly favored Bloch. Although Cowan and Bloch had negotiated only for the sale of an apartment building, the documents stated that Cowan was selling both the apartment house and his residence, which was located across the street from the apartments. The referee found that Cowan had no intention of selling his residence and did not know that it was included in the sale. It was unclear whether Belleville (D) knowingly participated in his client's activities or merely followed the client's instructions without question. Whatever the case, Belleville (D) drafted the documents to include Cowan's house in the sale, and Cowan signed the documents without realizing he was transferring title to his house. A referee recommended no discipline against Belleville (D) on the basis he owed no attorney-client obligation to Cowan. The Florida Bar (P) appealed the referee's decision.

ISSUE: Does an attorney have a duty to explain to an unrepresented opposing party the fact that the attorney is representing an adverse interest and the material terms of the documents involved?

HOLDING AND DECISION: (Per curiam) Yes. An attorney has a duty to explain to an unrepresented opposing party the fact that the attorney is representing an adverse interest and must explain the material terms of the documents involved. The record established that Cowan had negotiated to sell the apartment, that he did not intend to sell anything other than the apartment, and that he did not know that the documents of sale would result in the loss of his residence. Furthermore, Belleville (D) should have harbored suspicions about the documents he was preparing

because the documents established on their face a transaction so one-sided as to put Belleville (D) on notice of the likelihood of their uncon-scionability. When the transaction is as one-sided as that in the instant case, counsel preparing the documents is under an ethical duty to make sure that an unrepresented party understands the possible detrimental effect of the transaction and the fact that the attorney's loyalty lies with the client alone. Here Belleville (D) breached that duty. The no discipline recommendation of the referee is reversed, and Belleville (D) is suspended from the practice of law for thirty days.

▶ ANALYSIS

As the *Belleville* decision makes clear, an attorney must avoid the appearance of simultaneously representing adverse interests, especially where the opposing party may be unfairly induced to rely on the attorney's advice or skill in preparing legal documents.

■=■

Quicknotes

ATTORNEY-CLIENT PRIVILEGE A doctrine precluding the admission into evidence of confidential communications between an attorney and his client made in the course of obtaining professional assistance.

■=■

Lawyers for Companies and Other Organizations

Quick Reference Rules of Law

Tekni-Plex, Inc. v. Meyner & Landis

Manufacturing and packing corporation (P) v. Attorneys (D)

N.Y. Ct. App., 89 N.Y.2d 123, 674 N.E.2d 663 (1996).

NATURE OF CASE: Appeal over a corporate acquisition involving counsel's duties to the company and its sole shareowner.

FACT SUMMARY: Tang wanted to retain the same counsel his old corporation used after he had sold the corporation to another company. The new owners sought to disqualify this counsel.

🏛 RULE OF LAW
Counsel cannot represent a present client against a former client involving matters that are substantially related to the prior representation and where the interests of the present client are materially adverse to the interests of the former client.

FACTS: Tom Tang was the president, chief executive officer, sole director, and sole shareholder of Tekni-Plex, Inc. Meyner & Landis (M&L) (D) represented Tang and Tekni-Plex on various legal matters, including securing an environmental permit for the operation of a laminator machine. Tang agreed to sell Tekni-Plex to the TP Acquisition Company (Acquisition). Acquisition was a shell corporation whose sole purpose was for the purchase of Tekni-Plex. Once the two corporations are merged, Tekni-Plex would cease to exist and Acquisition would change its name to Tekni-Plex, Inc. (new Tekni-Plex) (P). Tang represented that old Tekni-Plex was in full compliance with all applicable environmental laws and possessed all requisite environmental permits. Tang and old Tekni-Plex was responsible for indemnification for any losses incurred by Acquisition as a result of misrepresentation. Following the merger, new Tekni-Plex (P) claimed that a laminator machine emitted volatile organic compounds and was therefore not allowed to operate. New Tekni-Plex (P) brought a claim against Tang for indemnification and Tang retained M&L (D) as counsel. New Tekni-Plex (P) sought to enjoin M&L (D) from representing Tang.

ISSUE: Can a long-time counsel for the seller company and its sole shareholder continue to represent the shareholder in a dispute with the buyer?

HOLDING AND DECISION: (Kaye, C.J.) No. Counsel cannot represent an present client against a former client involving matters that are substantially related to the prior representation and where the interests of the present client are materially adverse to the interests of the former client. The court ruled that new Tekni-Plex (P) had the burden of satisfying a three pronged test for the disqualification of M&L (D). First, the court found that new Tekni-Plex (P) is a former client of M&L (D) since following the merger, the business of old Tekni-Plex remained unchanged and consequently control of the attorney-client privilege passed to the hands of the new Tekni-Plex (P) management. Second, the court found that there was a substantial relationship between the current and former representations since the current dispute concerned the merger agreement on which the law firm had represented old Tekni-Plex. Third, the court concluded that the interests of M&L's (D) present (Tang) client were materially adverse to the interests of its former client (Tekni-Plex) because the claim set the purchaser's interest against Tang's interest as the seller. Because of the inherent conflicts of interest, M&L (D) were disqualified from representing Tang.

▶ ANALYSIS

Although the court found that new Tekni-Plex (P) is a former client of M&L (D) since it is essentially the same as old Tekni-Plex, they prohibited M&L (D) from releasing certain communications to new Tekni-Plex (P). These communications included Tang's confidences to M&L (D) during the merger negotiations. Giving new Tekni-Plex (P) this information would cause a chilling effect between attorneys and their clients since clients would worry that their privileged communications with counsel might later become available to others.

■═■

Quicknotes

ATTORNEY-CLIENT PRIVILEGE A doctrine precluding the admission into evidence of confidential communications between an attorney and his client made in the course of obtaining professional assistance.

CONFLICT OF INTEREST Refers to ethical problems that arise, or may be anticipated to arise, between an attorney and his client if the interests of the attorney, another client or a third party conflict with those of the present client.

DISQUALIFICATION A determination of unfitness or ineligibility.

■═■

In re Grand Jury Subpoena

n/a

415 F.3d 333 (4th Cir. 2005).

NATURE OF CASE: Appeal from denial of motion to quash grand jury subpoenas.

FACT SUMMARY: Former employees of AOL contended that grand jury subpoenas for documents related to an internal investigation conducted by AOL's attorneys should be quashed because the requested documents were protected by the attorney-client privilege and the joint defense privilege.

🏛 RULE OF LAW
(1) Conversations between a corporate employee and a corporation's attorneys during an internal investigation are not protected by the attorney-client privilege where the employee cannot show that an attorney-client relationship was formed during the investigation.
(2) Conversations between a corporate employee and a corporation's attorneys during an internal investigation are not protected by the joint defense privilege where the employee has entered into a common interest agreement with the company following the investigation.

FACTS: From March through June 2001, AOL conducted an internal investigation into its relationship with PurchasePro, Inc. Outside counsel as well as in-house counsel conducted the investigation and interviewed AOL employees, including Wakeford, John Doe 1, and John Doe 2. The attorneys informed these employees that they represented AOL; that although the conversations were privileged, AOL could waive the privilege; and, if there was a conflict, the attorney-client privilege belonged to AOL. The attorneys also told the employees either that they could represent them, barring a conflict, or that the employees could retain their own counsel, at AOL expense. In November, the Securities Exchange Commission (SEC) began to investigate AOL's relationship with PurchasePro. In December 2001, Wakeford and AOL, through counsel, entered into a "common interest agreement," which in part indicated that the disclosure of "Common Interest Materials" would not diminish the confidentiality of those materials or waive any applicable privilege. The employees testified before the SEC in 2002, and at their hearings, when questioned about their discussions with AOL attorneys during the March-June 2001 internal investigation, claimed that those discussions were protected by the attorney-client privilege. The employees indicated that they believed they were represented by the attorneys during those interviews. Two years later, a federal grand jury issued a subpoena commanding AOL to provide written memoranda and other written records reflecting the interviews of the employees conducted by the AOL attorneys from March to

June 2001. AOL agreed to waive the attorney-client privilege and produce the subpoenaed documents, but the employees moved to quash the subpoena on the grounds that they each had an individual attorney-client relationship with the investigating attorneys, that their interviews were individually privileged, and that they had not waived the privilege. Wakeford also claimed that the information he disclosed to the investigating attorneys was privileged under the common interest doctrine. The district court denied the motions to quash, finding that in the case of all three employees, none were clients of the investigating attorneys at the time of the interviews, and also denied Wakeford's motion on the ground that his common interest agreement with AOL postdated the interviews. The court based its conclusion on its findings that: (1) the investigating attorneys told them that they represented the company; (2) the investigating attorneys told them, "we represent you," not "we do represent you"; (3) they could not show that the investigating attorneys agreed to represent them; and (4) the investigating attorneys told them that the attorney-client privilege belonged to AOL and AOL could choose to waive it. The court of appeals granted review.

ISSUE:
(1) Are conversations between a corporate employee and a corporation's attorneys during an internal investigation protected by the attorney-client privilege where the employee cannot show that an attorney-client relationship was formed during the investigation?
(2) Are conversations between a corporate employee and a corporation's attorneys during an internal investigation protected by the joint defense privilege where the employee has entered into a common interest agreement with the company following the investigation?

HOLDING AND DECISION: (Wilson, J.)
(1) No. Conversations between a corporate employee and a corporation's attorneys during an internal investigation are not protected by the attorney-client privilege where the employee cannot show that an attorney-client relationship was formed during the investigation. The essential elements for the formation of an attorney-client relationship between the investigating attorneys and the employees were missing at the time of the interviews. Despite the employees' subjective belief that the attorneys were representing them personally, there was no evidence of an objectively reasonable, mutual understanding that the employees were seeking legal advice from the attorneys or that the attorneys were rendering personal legal advice. This conclusion is supported by the attorneys' disclosure

Continued on next page.

to the employees that they represented AOL, and that the privilege and the right to waive it were AOL's alone. Moreover, the attorneys' statement to the employees that they could represent them absent a conflict was not a statement that they were representing them. In general, an individual's subjective belief that he is represented is not alone sufficient to create an attorney-client relationship. Instead, that subjective belief must be reasonable under the circumstances. Here, under the circumstances, the employees could not reasonably have believed that the investigating attorneys were representing them, given the attorneys' explicit disclaimers about AOL being their client, that the privilege belonged to AOL alone, and that they could, in theory represent the employees (which in itself suggests that they were not representing the employees at the time of the interviews). In addition, the employees never asked the attorneys to represent them, nor did the attorneys offer to do so. Therefore, the district court did not err in finding that no attorney-client relationship was established at the time of the investigation, and, accordingly, the employees do not have a privilege that they can assert. Affirmed as to this issue.

(2) No. Conversations between a corporate employee and a corporation's attorneys during an internal investigation are not protected by the joint defense privilege where the employee has entered into a common interest agreement with the company following the investigation. The joint defense privilege is an extension of the attorney-client privilege, and serves to protect communications between parties who share a common interest in litigation. The purpose of the privilege is to allow persons with a common interest to communicate with their respective attorneys and with each other to more effectively prosecute or defend their claims. For the privilege to apply, the proponent must establish that the parties had "some common interest about a legal matter." An employee's cooperation in an internal investigation alone is not sufficient to establish a common interest; rather "some form of joint strategy is necessary." The common interest agreement between AOL and Wakeford did not exist prior to December 2001, and these parties were not pursuing a joint legal strategy before that time. Also, during the time of the internal investigation, AOL would not have known whether its interests were aligned with, or adverse to, those of Wakeford. Accordingly, the district court did not err in concluding that Wakeford did not have a joint defense privilege during the investigation or any time before December 2001. Affirmed as to this issue.

▶ ANALYSIS

If the investigating attorneys had in fact entered into an attorney-client relationship with the employees, they would not have been free to waive the employees' privilege when a conflict arose, since ethically they could not place one client's interests above those of another. Rather, the attorneys would

have had to withdraw from all representation and to maintain all confidences. As the court itself observes, investigating counsel would not have been able to robustly investigate and report to management or the board of directors of a publicly-traded corporation with the necessary candor if it were constrained by ethical obligations to individual employees. It is exactly for this reason that courts are reluctant to find that investigating attorneys who interview corporate employees or other corporate constituents form an attorney-client relationship with those interviewed. If they did, the investigating attorney would be faced with multiple conflicts and would be immobilized from conducting an investigation into wrongdoing.

■■■

Quicknotes

ATTORNEY-CLIENT PRIVILEGE A doctrine precluding the admission into evidence of confidential communications between an attorney and his client made in the course of obtaining professional assistance.

ATTORNEY-CLIENT RELATIONSHIP The confidential relationship established when a lawyer enters into employment with a client.

QUASH To vacate, annul, void.

SUBPOENA A command issued by court to compel a witness to appear at trial.

■■■

Murphy & Demory, Ltd., et al. v. Admiral Daniel J. Murphy, U.S.N. (Ret.), et al.

Corporation (P) v. Former co-owner of corporation (D)

C.C. Va., Chancery No. 128219 (1994).

NATURE OF CASE: Legal malpractice action.

FACT SUMMARY: After Pillsbury (D), the law firm representing Murphy & Demory, Ltd. (P), assisted co-owner Murphy (D) in his efforts to take control of Murphy & Demory (P), Murphy & Demory (P) sued Pillsbury (D) for legal malpractice.

🏛 **RULE OF LAW**
Where dual representation of both a corporation and its individual owners presents a conflict of interest, the attorneys must obtain the corporation's consent for such representation after full disclosure of all material facts.

FACTS: Admiral Murphy (D) and Demory (P) co-owned Murphy & Demory, Ltd. (P). The law firm for Murphy & Demory, Ltd. (P), Pillsbury, Madison & Sutro (D), through its attorneys Siemer (D) and Mendelson (D) assisted Murphy (D) in his efforts to take control of Murphy & Demory (P) or to form, before resigning from the company, a new corporation to compete with Murphy & Demory (P). Pillsbury (D) ignored its junior associates' warnings that the dual representation was rife with conflicts of interest, with possible breaches of fiduciary duty, and use of corporate opportunities. Murphy & Demory (P) filed suit against Admiral Murphy (D) and against Pillsbury (D).

ISSUE: Where dual representation of both a corporation and its individual owners presents a conflict of interest, must the attorneys obtain the corporation's consent for such representation after full disclosure of all material facts?

HOLDING AND DECISION: (Roush, J.) Yes. Where dual representation of both a corporation and its individual owners presents a conflict of interest, the attorneys must obtain the corporation's consent for such representation after full disclosure of all material facts. Here, Pillsbury (D) failed to disclose the conflict, to obtain consent for the dual representation of both Murphy (D) and Murphy & Demory, Ltd. (P), or, failing that, to withdraw from the representation. In concluding that there was no conflict, Siemer (D) willfully ignored the Rules of Professional Conduct. As a direct and proximate result of Pillsbury's (D) legal malpractice, Murphy & Demory, Ltd. (P) suffered compensatory damages in the amount of $500,000, and judgment is entered for that amount, along with interest.

▶ **ANALYSIS**

The court was particularly disturbed by the fact that every inquiry by an associate into the propriety of the firm's actions was referred to Siemer (D) for resolution. Siemer (D), the partner in charge of the client relationship affected by the issue, was the least likely to be objective, yet she was the ultimate arbiter of whether the firm had a conflict of interest. Mendelson (D) was held equally responsible for the legal malpractice since he was senior enough to have put a stop to the undisclosed dual representation.

■■■

Quicknotes

CONFLICT OF INTEREST Refers to ethical problems that arise, or may be anticipated to arise, between an attorney and his client if the interests of the attorney, another client or a third party conflict with those of the present client.

FIDUCIARY DUTY A legal obligation to act for the benefit of another, including subordinating one's personal interests to that of the other person.

■■■

Crews v. Buckman Laboratories International, Inc.

Discharged attorney (P) v. Employer (D)

Tenn. Sup. Ct., 78 S.W.3d 852 (2002).

NATURE OF CASE: Appeal from the dismissal of a complaint.

FACT SUMMARY: When Buckman Laboratories International, Inc. (D) discharged Crews (P), an at-will in-house lawyer, for reporting that her supervisor was engaging in the unauthorized practice of law, Crews (P) sued Buckman Laboratories (D) for retaliatory discharge in violation of public policy.

🏛 RULE OF LAW
An in-house lawyer can sue her employer for retaliatory discharge for reporting the employer's violation of mandatory ethical duties.

FACTS: In 1995, Crews (P) was hired by Buckman Laboratories nternational, Inc. (D) as in-house associate general counsel in its legal department, reporting to Buckman Laboratories'(D) general counsel, Katherine Davis. The employment relationship was at-will. In 1996, Crews (P) discovered that Davis, who held herself out as a licensed attorney, did not in fact possess a license to practice law in Tennessee. When Crews (P) reported this to the state bar, Buckman Laboratories (D) summarily terminated her. Crews (P) sued Buckman Laboratories (D), alleging a common-law action for retaliatory discharge in violation of public policy. The trial court dismissed the complaint for failure to state a valid claim. The intermediate appellate court affirmed, and Crews (P) appealed.

ISSUE: May an in-house lawyer sue her employer for retaliatory discharge for reporting the employer's violation of mandatory ethical duties?

HOLDING AND DECISION: (Barker, J.) Yes. An in-house lawyer can sue her employer for retaliatory discharge for reporting the employer's violation of mandatory ethical duties. Although usually the employment at-will doctrine permits the employer or employee to terminate the employment relationship at their discretion, an at-will employee generally may not be discharged for attempting to exercise a statutory or constitutional right, or for any other reason which violates a clear public policy which is evidenced by an unambiguous constitutional, statutory, or regulatory provision. This court accepts the position of California, Massachusetts, and Montana that a lawyer is generally permitted to assert a retaliatory discharge action if the lawyer is discharged for following a mandatory ethical duty or engaging in conduct that would give rise to an action by a non-lawyer employee. Since the very purpose of recognizing an employee's action for retaliatory discharge in violation of public policy is to encourage the employee to protect the public interest, it would be anomolous to protect only non-lawyer employees under these circumstances. Indeed, in-house counsel do not forfeit employment protections provided to other employees merely because of their status or duties as a lawyer. Clearly, the bar's disciplinary rules place upon lawyers a mandatory ethical duty not to aid a non-lawyer in the unauthorized practice of law. Here, even though Crews (P) was not under a mandatory ethical duty to report her superior's unauthorized practice of law, she certainly possessed a permissive duty to report such conduct. Reversed.

▶ ANALYSIS

As pointed out in the *Crews* decision, the pressure to conform to corporate misconduct presents a definite risk that ethical standards could be disregarded and that, while in-house counsel may be a lawyer, courts must further recognize that he or she is also an employee of the corporation, with all of the attendant benefits and responsibilities.

■■■

Quicknotes

ATTORNEY-CLIENT PRIVILEGE A doctrine precluding the admission into evidence of confidential communications between an attorney and his client made in the course of obtaining professional assistance.

CONFLICT OF INTEREST Refers to ethical problems that arise, or may be anticipated to arise, between an attorney and his client if the interests of the attorney, another client or a third party conflict with those of the present client.

FIDUCIARY DUTY A legal obligation to act for the benefit of another, including subordinating one's personal interests to that of the other person.

RETALIATORY DISCHARGE The firing of an employee in retribution for an act committed against the employer's interests.

■■■

Judges

Quick Reference Rules of Law

Liljeberg v. Health Services Acquisition Corp.

Businessman (P) v. Corporation (D)

486 U.S. 847 (1988).

NATURE OF CASE: Review of order vacating judgment upon judge's failure to recuse.

FACT SUMMARY: A judge discovered, after he had rendered a verdict but before judgment became final, that he had a personal interest in the litigation.

🏛 RULE OF LAW
A judge, upon discovering a personal interest in a litigation, must recuse himself any time before final entry of judgment.

FACTS: A contractual dispute arose between Liljeberg (P) and Health Services Acquisition Corp. (D) over the right to construct a hospital. Loyola University stood to benefit if Liljeberg (P) won. The judge to whom the case was assigned was a trustee of Loyola, although he apparently was unaware of Loyola's interest in Liljeberg's (P) success. After a bench trial, the judge announced a verdict in favor of Liljeberg (P). Several days later, before final entry of judgment, Loyola's interest was brought to the judge's attention. He denied a motion to vacate, and he entered judgment. The court of appeals reversed, holding that the judge should have recused himself immediately upon discovery of his interest. Liljeberg (P) petitioned for certiorari.

ISSUE: Must a judge, upon discovering personal interest in a litigation, recuse himself any time before final entry of judgment?

HOLDING AND DECISION: (Stevens, J.) Yes. A judge, upon discovering a personal interest in a litigation, must recuse himself any time before final entry of judgment. 28 U.S.C. § 455 provides that a judge shall disqualify himself in any proceeding in which his impartiality might be questioned. The section goes on to list a personal financial interest as a reason for such disqualification. Ill will or scienter is not a requirement for recusal; the section is designed to avoid even the appearance of bias. While a judge obviously cannot recuse himself for something he does not know, if such knowledge is imparted to him any time during the course of the action, a pall is cast over the whole proceeding, as such important motions as requests for new trials might be made right up to the time of final entry. For a judge to rule on such items with knowledge of a personal interest would undermine public confidence in the judiciary, an eventuality § 455 was drafted to prevent. Affirmed.

DISSENT: (Rehnquist, C.J.) The Court has used § 455 as a vehicle to compel judges to disqualify themselves for facts they do not know. It also broadens the standard for vacating final judgments under Fed. R. Civ. P. 60(b). These results are at odds with the intended scope of § 455 and Rule 60(b), and invite considerable mischief when courts attempt to apply them.

DISSENT: (O'Connor, J.) Constructive knowledge cannot be a basis for a § 455 violation.

▶ ANALYSIS

The Court's ruling appears to have been broader in scope than necessary. In dicta, the Court seemed to say that § 455 encompasses a "should have known" standard. In this particular instance, the judge did acquire actual knowledge. The dissents took the Court to task for its broad holding.

■═■

Quicknotes

28 U.S.C. § 455 A judge must recuse himself in any proceeding in which his impartiality might be questioned.

■═■

In re Marriage of Iverson

n/a

Cal. Ct. App., 11 Cal. App. 4th 1495, 15 Cal. Rptr. 2d 70 (1992).

NATURE OF CASE: Appeal from judgment dividing property pursuant to a marital dissolution.

FACT SUMMARY: A trial judge, in his opinion accompanying a property division decree, cited stereotypical notions in explaining how he arrived at his decision.

🏛 RULE OF LAW
A judicial ruling cannot be based on stereotypical notions of gender.

FACTS: The Iversons divorced. George Iverson (D) was an influential individual in the entertainment industry. Cheryl Iverson (P) challenged the validity of an antenuptial agreement she had signed prior to the marriage. Cheryl (P) testified that she had not known what she was signing; George (D) testified that she had been fully informed about the nature of the document. The trial judge held the agreement valid, but did order George (D) to maintain a life insurance policy favoring Cheryl (P). The order was accompanied by an opinion that used some thinly disguised language indicating that Cheryl (P) had been gold-digging in her relationship with George (D), and that she had been little more than a trophy wife to him. Constant references to Cheryl's (P) physical qualities were made in the opinion, and she was referred to as a "girl," although she was in her forties. Both parties appealed.

ISSUE: Can a judicial ruling be based on stereotypical notions of gender?

HOLDING AND DECISION: (Sills, J.) No. A judicial decision cannot be based on stereotypical notions of gender. A trial must be both fair and appear to be fair. Acts or words by a judge that show that his ruling is based not on individualized facts but on group notions does not meet this standard. Here, the trial court seems to have cited stereotypical notions of wealthy older men and attractive younger women as the basis for his decision, and this type of stereotyping cannot be condoned. Reversed. [The court then directed the presiding judge of the trial court to disqualify the trial judge from hearing the retrial.]

CONCURRENCE: (Moore, J.) It is doubtful that there was actual bias here, but there was an appearance of bias sufficient to warrant reversal.

▶ ANALYSIS

An attorney is under a duty to avoid not only conflicts of interest, but appearances of conflict as well. As the present case illustrates, the same is true for judges. The appearance of improper bases for a decision may in itself be sufficient to disqualify a judge from hearing a case.

■■■

Quicknotes

IMPARTIALITY The neutral demeanor of the tribunal or the trier-of-fact when adjudicating a dispute.

■■■

Matter of Bourisseau

n/a

Mich. Sup. Ct., 439 Mich. 1230, 480 N.W.2d 270 (1992).

NATURE OF CASE: Order of discipline of a judge following the findings of a judicial tenure committee.

FACT SUMMARY: After Judge Bourisseau (D) made remarks which were widely disseminated in the news media and were criticized as insensitive and racist, the Judicial Tenure Commission recommended that he be disciplined.

🏛 RULE OF LAW
Public remarks made by a judge which are racially offensive and improper constitute misconduct in office.

FACTS: During a newspaper interview, Judge Bourisseau (D) was asked for his views on the Parental Rights Restoration Act. Judge Bourisseau (D) expressed his displeasure with the enactment of the Act and stated that he might permit a white minor to have an abortion if she were raped by a black man. Those remarks were widely disseminated in the news media. Several grievances were filed with the Judicial Tenure Commission. Judge Bourisseau (D) indicated it had not been his intention to speak in a racially insensitive manner and expressed regret for his remarks. The Commission recommended an order of discipline. In issuing the order, the court followed the findings of the Commission.

ISSUE: Do public remarks made by a judge which are racially offensive and improper constitute misconduct in office?

HOLDING AND DECISION: [Judge not stated in casebook excerpt.] Yes. Public remarks made by a judge which are racially offensive and improper constitute misconduct in office. Judge Bourisseau's (D) remarks called into question the impartiality of the judiciary and exposed the judicial system to contempt and ridicule. Such erosion of public confidence in the judiciary is clearly prejudicial to the administration of justice. Thus, a public censure is an appropriate response to Judge Bourisseau's (D) remarks. Affirmed.

▶ ANALYSIS

Section 3(B)(5) of the Code of Judicial Conduct requires a judge to "perform judicial duties without bias or prejudice." A judge is forbidden, in the performance of those duties, to manifest bias or prejudice by words or conduct or to permit staff, court officials, and others subject to the judge's direction and control to do so. In addition, § 2(C) of the 1990 Code states that "A judge shall not hold membership in any organization that practices invidious discrimination on the basis of race, sex, religion or national origin." Further, the limitation imposed on the speech of judges, in § 3(B)(9), is broader than any limitation the First Amendment would tolerate for others.

■━■

Quicknotes

IMPARTIALITY The neutral demeanor of the tribunal or the trier-of-fact when adjudicating a dispute.

■━■

CHAPTER 12

Control of Quality: Reducing the Likelihood of Professional Failure

Quick Reference Rules of Law

Supreme Court of New Hampshire v. Piper

Supreme Court of New Hampshire (D) v. Vermont resident (P)

470 U.S. 274 (1985).

NATURE OF CASE: Review of order invalidating residency requirement for admission to state bar.

FACT SUMMARY: New Hampshire Supreme Court's (D) rule limiting attorney admissions to state residents was attacked as unconstitutional.

🏛 RULE OF LAW
A state may not limit attorney admissions to its residents.

FACTS: Piper (P) was a Vermont resident living near the border with New Hampshire. New Hampshire's Supreme Court (D) limited New Hampshire attorney admissions to residents only. Piper (P) applied to take the New Hampshire bar examination. Informed of the residency requirement, she said that she would undertake New Hampshire residency if she passed the bar exam. She did pass but requested an exemption to the residency requirement. This was denied. She then filed an action in federal court, contending that the residency requirement violated the privileges and immunities clause of Article IV, § 2 of the Constitution. The district court held the rule unconstitutional, and the court of appeals affirmed. The U.S. Supreme Court granted certiorari.

ISSUE: May a state limit attorney admissions to its residents?

HOLDING AND DECISION: (Powell, J.) No. A state may not limit attorney admissions to its residents. The privileges and immunities clause guarantees that each state will grant citizens of other states the same rights as enjoyed by its citizens. Since the clause was intended to fuse into one nation a collection of states, this Court has ruled that such activities that bear on the vitality of the nation as a single entity are those covered by the clause. Economic activity has particularly been held to be covered by the clause. The practice of law is without doubt an economic activity, and would naturally seem to fall within the clause. New Hampshire Supreme Court (D) argues that the practice of law is so bound up with a state's judiciary and administration of justice it should be exempted from the clause. However, a lawyer is not a state officer in the ordinary understanding of the term, being his own agent and making his own decisions. Therefore, the clause must apply to the practice of law. This being so, a state must demonstrate a substantial reason for disparate treatment. Here, New Hampshire's Supreme Court (D) argues that non-local attorneys are less likely to be familiar with local laws and procedure, behave ethically, be available, and do pro bono work. No proof of this has been put forward and this Court remains skeptical. Affirmed.

CONCURRENCE: (White, J.) The residency requirement is invalid as applied to Piper (P).

DISSENT: (Rehnquist, J.) The Court's decision clearly disregards the fact that the practice of law is—almost by definition—fundamentally different from other forms of economic activity practiced across state lines. In fact, certain aspects of legal practice are distinctly and intentionally non-rational; in this regard, one might view the legal system as the antithesis of the norms embodied in the privileges and immunities clause.

▶ ANALYSIS

Not all activities which cross state lines come within the ambit of the clause. Those activities not bearing on the vitality of the nation as a whole are not. An example of this was *Baldwin v. Fish and Game Commission*, 436 U.S. 371 (1978). In that case disparate treatment with respect to hunting licenses was upheld.

■=■

Quicknotes

U.S. CONSTITUTION, ARTICLE IV, § 2 U.S. CONSTITUTION "The citizens of each state shall be entitled to all privileges and immunities of citizens in the several states."

■=■

Supreme Court of Virginia v. Friedman

Supreme Court (D) v. Non-resident attorney (P)

487 U.S. 59 (1988).

NATURE OF CASE: Review of order invalidating state residency requirements for reciprocal bar admissions.

FACT SUMMARY: The Virginia Supreme Court (D) permitted attorneys licensed to practice in other states to practice in Virginia without taking the bar examination, provided that they resided in Virginia.

🏛 RULE OF LAW
A state may not make residency a condition for reciprocal bar admission.

FACTS: The Virginia Supreme Court (D) offered an exemption to passing the state bar examination for attorneys already admitted in other jurisdictions to practice in Virginia. One condition of this exemption was residency in Virginia, the others being full-time practice in Virginia and licensure in a state offering reciprocal rights. Friedman (P) lived in Maryland but wished to practice full-time in Virginia, where she had formerly lived. Maryland provided an examination waiver similar to that of Virginia. Friedman (P) applied for Virginia's waiver but was denied the waiver due to non-residency. Friedman (P) challenged the residency restriction in district court as a violation of the privileges and immunities clause of Article IV, § 2 of the Constitution. The district court enjoined enforcement of the requirement, and the Virginia Supreme Court (D) appealed. The court of appeals affirmed, and the Supreme Court granted certiorari.

ISSUE: May a state make residency a condition for reciprocal bar admission?

HOLDING AND DECISION: (Kennedy, J.) No. A state may not make residency a condition for reciprocal bar admission. The privileges and immunities clause of Article IV, § 2 requires states to put citizens of other states on an equal footing with citizens of the situs state with respect to activities bearing on the vitality of the nation as a whole. If an activity does bear on the nation as a single unit, any disparate treatment must serve a substantial state interest. The privileges and immunities clause has been particularly applied to economic activities and has been applied by this Court to the practice of law. The Virginia Supreme Court (D) argued that its rule did not categorically exclude practice in Virginia and therefore did not run afoul of the clause. However, this Court has never ruled that disparate treatment for purposes of the clause must amount to total exclusion and does not do so now. Having concluded that the clause is applicable to the treatment here, it must be shown that a substantial interest is served. The Court (D) argued that the interests served include insuring familiarity with Virginia law and that the attorney will fulfill his civic duties as an attorney. This Court is not prepared to agree that mere non-residency will prevent an otherwise qualified attorney from fulfilling his ethical obligation to be apprised of the law where he practices. Further, the requirement that the attorney practice full-time in Virginia would make this an unlikely scenario. Since the Court (D) cannot justify the residency requirement as serving a substantial interest, it cannot survive constitutional scrutiny. Affirmed.

DISSENT: (Rehnquist, C.J.) It was improper analysis that led the Court to invalidate a per se residency rule in *Supreme Court of New Hampshire v. Piper*, 470 U.S. 274 (1985), and the Court extends its flawed reasoning here. Beyond that, the Court has penalized Virginia for at least going part way to accommodate our increasingly mobile society. The unfortunate result of this decision will be the end to bar examination waivers across the nation.

▶ ANALYSIS

As stated above, a residency requirement for practice of law was invalidated in *Piper*, which essentially controlled the decision here. The Virginia Supreme Court (D), constrained by this decision, attempted to distinguish it by noting that its rule was not a blanket prohibition on practice. This argument was rejected.

Quicknotes

ARTICLE IV, § 2 U.S. CONSTITUTION "The citizens of each state shall be entitled to all privileges and immunities of citizens in the several states."

In re Mustafa

n/a

631 A.2d 45 (D.C. 1993).

NATURE OF CASE: Court action on the recommendation of the Committee on Admissions as to the fitness of a candidate for admissibility to the Bar.

FACT SUMMARY: Although Mustafa (D) embezzled moot court funds while in law school, the Committee on Admissions recommended that he be admitted to the D.C. Bar.

🏛 RULE OF LAW
In order to gain admission to the Bar, an applicant must demonstrate by clear and convincing evidence that he possesses good moral character and general fitness to practice law at the time of admission.

FACTS: While in law school, Mustafa (D) shared with Brennan access to and control over the checking account for the law school's moot court program. During a five-month period, he wrote thirteen checks for his own use, totaling $4,331. After Mustafa (D) gave Brennan a cashier's check for $2,200, Brennan disclosed Mustafa's (D) misconduct to the law school dean. On the same day, Mustafa (D) confessed his misconduct to a law school professor and to the Committee on Admissions. Following a hearing, the Committee found that Mustafa (D) always intended to repay the sums taken from the fund and had made full restitution before there was any threatened action by the law school. The Committee unanimously recommended that Mustafa (D) be admitted to the D.C. Bar.

ISSUE: In order to gain admission to the Bar, must an applicant demonstrate by clear and convincing evidence that he possesses good moral character and general fitness to practice law at the time of admission?

HOLDING AND DECISION: (Sullivan, J.) Yes. In order to gain admission to the Bar, an applicant must demonstrate by clear and convincing evidence that he possesses good moral character and general fitness to practice law at the time of admission. Its recommendation notwithstanding, the Committee found that Mustafa's (D) conduct "could be considered criminal in nature and would almost invariably have resulted in the disbarment of an attorney admitted to practice." It appears likely that Mustafa (D) will be able to establish the requisite good moral character at some future time. However, given the relatively short period of time that has elapsed since the date of his misconduct, Mustafa (D) has failed to establish that he has the good moral character required for admission to the Bar. Accordingly, his application is denied.

▶ ANALYSIS

While criminal conduct has traditionally excluded Bar applicants, a felony conviction automatically disqualifies an applicant in only eight jurisdictions. In making a decision regarding admission, other jurisdictions consider factors such as the nature of the crime, how long ago it occurred, and the conduct of the applicant since then. Lack of candor in the application process and cheating on examinations can also bar admission, as can mental health, financial probity, and an applicant's private life.

Quicknotes

FIDUCIARY DUTY A legal obligation to act for the benefit of another, including subordinating one's personal interests to that of the other person.

Leis v. Flynt

Ohio judges (D) v. Magazine publisher (P)

439 U.S. 438 (1979).

NATURE OF CASE: Review of order enjoining criminal prosecution.

FACT SUMMARY: Out-of-state counsel for Flynt (P) contended that a state court's summary denial of their request to appear pro hac vice was unconstitutional.

🏛 RULE OF LAW
Absent a governing rule or statute, a summary denial of a request to appear pro hac vice is not unconstitutional.

FACTS: Flynt (P) was charged in an Ohio state court with various criminal acts in connection with distribution of his Hustler magazine. Flynt (P) retained Fahringer and Cambria as counsel, neither of whom were admitted to practice in Ohio. They requested admission pro hac vice. Ohio had no governing law or rule regarding pro hac vice admission. The trial court summarily denied the request, and the Ohio Supreme Court denied mandamus. Flynt (P) filed an action in federal district court, contending that the summary denial was unconstitutional and requesting that prosecution be enjoined. The district court enjoined the prosecution until such time as the trial court held a hearing based on clear legal standards. The Sixth Circuit affirmed, and the Supreme Court granted certiorari.

ISSUE: Is a summary denial of a request to appear pro hac vice unconstitutional absent a governing rule or statute?

HOLDING AND DECISION: (Per curiam) No. Absent a governing rule or statute, a summary denial of a request to appear pro hac vice is not unconstitutional. The Constitution does not create property interests; rather, it guarantees due process protection to rights created elsewhere. In the context of this case, the right to practice pro hac vice cannot be created by the Constitution, such right must arise elsewhere. In Ohio, there is no law or rule governing pro hac vice admissions. Consequently, there is no source of a substantive right to practice that the Constitution might protect. This being so, Flynt's (P) due process argument with respect to pro hac vice admission fails. Reversed and remanded.

DISSENT: (Stevens, J.) An attorney has a property interest in pursuing his calling. A state may not arbitrarily deny an out-of-state attorney the right to practice law in its courts. The denial of Flynt's (P) counsels' request bore no rational relationship to the goal of guaranteeing professional competence.

▶ ANALYSIS

Pro hac vice admissions are becoming more and more commonplace. This is a reflection of several trends in the law. Increasing specialization has led to the demand for specialists to practice across state lines. Also, the trend toward "megafirms" which practice in many jurisdictions has tended to promote lawyer mobility.

■━■

Quicknotes

DUE PROCESS The constitutional mandate requiring the courts to protect and enforce individuals' rights and liberties consistent with prevailing principals of fairness and justice and prohibiting the federal and state governments from such activities that deprive its citizens of a life, liberty or property interest.

PRO HAC VICE Applicable to a specific occasion; the use or application of a condition for the limited duration of a single situation.

■━■

Birbrower, Montalbano, Condon & Frank, P.C. v. Superior Court

Law firm (D/Petitioner), unlicensed in California, v. Court (Respondent); Corporation (P/Real Party in Interest)

17 Cal. 4th 119, 949 P.2d 1, 70 Cal. Rptr. 2d 304 (1998), cert. denied, 525 U.S. 920 (1998).

NATURE OF CASE: Appeal from judgment that law firm practiced law without a license and was therefore not entitled to collect under fee agreement.

FACT SUMMARY: Birbrower (D/Petitioner), a New York law firm unlicensed to practice law in California, performed legal services for ESQ (P/Real Party in Interest), a California-based corporation, without a license. ESQ (P) refused to pay, alleging malpractice and claiming that the firm could not collect its fee because of its unauthorized practice of law. Birbrower (D) counterclaimed for its fee.

RULE OF LAW
Advising a client and negotiating a settlement agreement in California without a license constitutes the unauthorized practice of law and no fee may be collected to the extent that the fee was for those services.

FACTS: ESQ (P/Real Party in Interest), a California corporation, retained Birbrower (D), a New York law firm. None of the firm's attorneys were licensed to practice law in California. The fee agreement was negotiated and executed in New York, but provided that California law would govern all matters related to the representation. During several trips to California, the Birbrower (D) attorneys met with ESQ (P) and its accountants, gave legal advice, and made recommendations. They also spoke on their client's behalf during settlement agreement negotiations. ESQ (P) alleged malpractice, and Birbrower (D), counterclaimed to recover its fee.

ISSUE: Does it constitute the unauthorized practice of law for a New York law firm, not licensed in California, to perform legal services in California for a California client under a fee agreement stating that California law will control?

HOLDING AND DECISION: (Chin, J.) Yes. The court noted that the legal definition of "practicing law" included the giving of legal advice and the preparation of legal documents. The court then turned to the question of the meaning of "in California," holding that an unlicensed lawyer must engage in quantitatively sufficient activities within California or create a continuing attorney-client relationship for it to be determined that the attorney "practiced law in California." Although physical presence within the state is a factor, the court did not include that as a requirement in its analysis. Ruling that Birbrower's (D) actions constituted the extensive practice of law in California, the court declined to permit the firm from collecting its fee to the extent that the fee was based on any of the work it performed while in California. Affirmed in part, and reversed and remanded in part.

DISSENT: (Kennard, J.) This judge would define "practicing law" in a more narrow way than the majority: "the representation of another in a judicial proceeding or an activity requiring the application of that degree of legal knowledge and technique possessed only by a trained legal mind." Because Birbrower's (D) activities while in California related only to arbitration, and arbitration is not necessarily "practicing law" under the above definition, the firm may have been entitled to relief.

ANALYSIS

The court recognized the distinction between the out-of-state litigator who obtains permission from a California judge to appear before that court pro hac vice and the out-of-state nonlitigator who cannot obtain similar authority to draft a legal document or provide legal advice to a client. Because case law offered no remedy for the nonlitigator who does not appear in a courtroom, the California legislature subsequently passed a law that permits, in effect, arbitrators the authority to admit out-of-state lawyers pro hac vice for in-state arbitrations.

Quicknotes

PRO HAC VICE Applicable to a specific occasion; the use or application of a condition for the limited duration of a single situation.

Professional Adjusters, Inc. v. Tandon

Insurance company (P) v. Insured fire victim (D)

Ind. Sup. Ct., 433 N.E.2d 779 (1982).

NATURE OF CASE: Appeal of dismissal of action for damages for breach of contract.

FACT SUMMARY: Professional Adjusters, Inc. (P) undertook to negotiate and adjust a claim on behalf of Tandon (D) against its insurer.

🏛 RULE OF LAW
Adjusting and negotiating a claim on behalf of an insured constitutes law practice.

FACTS: An Indiana statute permitted nonattorney adjusters to represent insureds in claims against insurers. At one point, Tandon (D) hired Professional Adjusters, Inc. (P) to negotiate a claim he was making against his carrier, U.S. Fidelity and Guaranty Co. (D). Subsequently, Tandon (D) contacted a lawyer, who sealed the claim. When Tandon (D) refused to pay the contingency fee to which he and Professional (P) had agreed, Professional (P) sued for breach of contract. Tandon (D) moved to dismiss on the grounds that the statute authorizing Professional (P) to represent him violated provisions in the state constitution prohibiting unauthorized law practice. The trial court agreed, holding the law unconstitutional and the fee agreement unenforceable. Professional (P) appealed.

ISSUE: Does adjusting and negotiating a claim on behalf of an insured constitute law practice?

HOLDING AND DECISION: (Pivarnik, J.) Yes. Adjusting and negotiating a claim on behalf of an insured constitutes law practice. Practicing law involves more than merely appearing in court. The core element of practicing law is the giving of advice to a client and the placing of oneself in the very sensitive position of being the client's repository of confidence with respect to managing his legal affairs. When a person undertakes to represent a person in a claim against that person's insurance company, he becomes the object of his client's trust and confidence. This, pure and simple, is law practice. Consequently, the statute authorizing representation by a nonlawyer violates the Indiana Constitution. Affirmed.

▌ ANALYSIS

Certain occupations involve activities that can border on law practice and have the potential for conflict with laws regarding unauthorized practice. Personal business managers are an example. Another example, probably the one encountered by the public most commonly, is the real estate agent.

CHAPTER 13

Control of Quality: Remedies for Professional Failure

Quick Reference Rules of Law

Togstad v. Vesely, Otto, Miller & Keefe

Paralysis victim (P) v. Law firm (D)

Minn. Sup. Ct., 291 N.W.2d 686 (1980).

NATURE OF CASE: Appeal of award of damages for legal malpractice.

FACT SUMMARY: Ms. Togstad (P) successfully sued Miller (D) of Vesely, Otto, Miller & Keefe (D) for legal malpractice, even though she had not formally retained him.

🏛 RULE OF LAW
A retainer is not required for an attorney-client relationship that may give rise to a malpractice claim to exist.

FACTS: Ms. Togstad (P) was rendered paralyzed after a medical procedure. Fourteen months later, Ms. Togstad (P) consulted with Miller (D) of Vesely, Otto, Miller & Keefe (D) regarding a possible malpractice action. After an initial consultation, Miller (D) informed Ms. Togstad (P) that he did not think she had a case, but that he would talk to his partners. Miller (D) never called back. After Minnesota's two-year statute of limitations on medical malpractice had expired, the Togstads (P) brought a legal malpractice action against Miller (D) for giving them erroneous advice and not advising them of the two-year statute. A jury found Miller (D) to have committed malpractice and awarded over $600,000 in damages. Miller (D) and his firm (D) appealed.

ISSUE: Is a retainer required for an attorney-client relationship that may give rise to a malpractice claim to exist?

HOLDING AND DECISION: (Per curiam) No. A retainer is not required for an attorney-client relationship that may give rise to a malpractice claim to exist. The first element in a malpractice claim is the existence of an attorney-client relationship. The crux of this relationship is the provision of advice by the attorney that he either knows or should know will be followed by the person to whom he provides the advice. This does not require actual retention. Here, Ms. Togstad (P) sought and obtained legal advice from Miller (D). It was entirely reasonable for Miller (D) to have expected the Togstads (P) to have followed his advice, which is exactly what they did. As a result, for purposes of a malpractice action, an attorney-client relationship between the Togstads (P) and Miller (D) existed. Affirmed.

▌ ANALYSIS

It is unclear as to whether the attorney-client relationship is defined by contract or tort theory. Appellate courts around the nation have gone both ways on this issue, on a variety of grounds. The court here recognized this diversity of opinion but did not indicate its preference for the one theory over the other. The court believed the contract and tort analyses for this case to be so similar that they did not need to be distinguished.

■══■

Quicknotes

ATTORNEY-CLIENT PRIVILEGE A doctrine precluding the admission into evidence of confidential communications between an attorney and his client made in the course of obtaining professional assistance.

RETAINER Compensation paid in advance for professional services.

■══■

Tante v. Herring

Attorney (D) v. Client seeking social security benefits (P)

Ga. Sup. Ct., 264 Ga. 694, 453 S.E.2d 686 (1994).

NATURE OF CASE: Action seeking damages against former counsel for legal malpractice, breach of fiduciary duty, and breach of contract.

FACT SUMMARY: Mrs. Herring (P) contended that Tante (D), her prior attorney, was liable for inducing her to have an affair with him.

🏛 RULE OF LAW
It is an actionable breach of fiduciary duty for an attorney to use information—available to him because of the attorney-client relationship—to his advantage and to the client's disadvantage.

FACTS: Tante (D) represented Mrs. Herring (P) in a Social Security Administration proceeding. During the course of his representation Mrs. Herring (P), who was married, had an affair with Tante (D). After the affair was over, the Herrings (P) sued Tante (D) for legal malpractice and breach of fiduciary duty, alleging that he used his knowledge of her fragile emotional state to induce her to have an affair, which had caused her emotional distress. The court of appeals held that the Herrings (P) could proceed on the breach of fiduciary duty claim. Tante (D) appealed.

ISSUE: Is it an actionable breach of fiduciary duty for an attorney to use information—available to him because of the attorney-client relationship—to his advantage and to the client's disadvantage?

HOLDING AND DECISION: (Hunt, C.J.) Yes. It is an actionable breach of fiduciary duty for an attorney to use information—available to him because of the attorney-client relationship—to his advantage and to the client's disadvantage. Even if Tante (D) was not guilty of malpractice in that his representation of Mrs. Herring (P) was competent, he still stands in a fiduciary relationship to her. If he used his superior knowledge to her detriment, he may be liable to the Herrings (P) for damages resulting from breach of the fiduciary duty to refrain from misusing confidential information. Acordingly, the Herrings (P) may pursue their claim. Affirmed.

▶ ANALYSIS

The problem encountered in this case presents several competing values. On the one hand, attorneys and their clients are consenting adults, who presumably have the capacity to make judgments about their relationships. On the other hand, the two are often unequal in terms of power, and the opportunity for exploitation is manifest. The states vary greatly as to how much leeway attorneys are given to engage in relationships with clients. Some prohibit it entirely. Others, like California, do not provide a blanket prohibition, but do not allow it in family law contexts, where a client may be particularly vulnerable emotionally.

■━■

Quicknotes

ATTORNEY-CLIENT PRIVILEGE A doctrine precluding the admission into evidence of confidential communications between an attorney and his client made in the course of obtaining professional assistance.

FIDUCIARY DUTY A legal obligation to act for the benefit of another, including subordinating one's personal interests to that of the other person.

■━■

Smith v. Haynsworth, Marion, McKay & Geurard

Real estate developer (P) v. Law firm (D)

S.C. Sup. Ct., 322 S.C. 433, 472 S.E.2d 612 (1996).

NATURE OF CASE: Appeal from defense verdict in malpractice action.

FACT SUMMARY: In a malpractice action against the legal firm Haynsworth, Marion, McKay & Geurard (D), the court excluded from evidence proffered testimony regarding violations of State Rules of Professional Conduct by the attorneys (D).

🏛 RULE OF LAW
Rules of Professional Conduct may be relevant in establishing legal malpractice.

FACTS: Smith (P) sued the firm Haynsworth, Marion, McKay & Geurard (D) over the latter's representation of him in a land development scheme that went sour. At trial, Smith (P) sought to introduce evidence that the firm (D) had violated state Rules of Professional Conduct. The court excluded this evidence. The jury returned a verdict in favor of Haynsworth, Marion, McKay & Geurard (D), and Smith (P) appealed.

ISSUE: May Rules of Professional Conduct be relevant in establishing legal malpractice?

HOLDING AND DECISION: (Waller, J.) Yes. Rules of Professional Conduct may be relevant in establishing legal malpractice. A plaintiff in a malpractice action must establish the standard of care that he alleges the attorney-defendant violated, and this must be done through expert testimony. Such an expert, generally an attorney or law professor, may rely on Rules of Professional Conduct as a standard by which to gauge the defendant's standard of conduct, so long as the rule whose violation is alleged was intended to protect a person in the position of the plaintiff. Here, the proffered testimony would appear to fall within this standard, so it should have been allowed. Reversed and remanded.

▌ ANALYSIS

States vary widely as to the extent to which they allow the use of rules of professional conduct to be used as a standard in malpractice actions. Some exclude them entirely, concluding that they are more prejudicial than probative. Others make their violation malpractice per se. The approach taken here could be described as a middle course between these two positions.

■═■

Quicknotes

EXPERT TESTIMONY Testimonial evidence about a complex area of subject matter relevant to trial, presented by a person competent to inform the trier of fact due to specialized knowledge or training.

LOCALITY A defined geographic region; the circumscribed location that defines the reach of a court's authority.

■═■

Hendry v. Pelland

Family involved in real estate transaction (P) v. Law firm (D)

73 F.3d 397 (D.C. Cir. 1996).

NATURE OF CASE: Appeal from judgment dismissing action seeking disgorgement of attorney fees.

FACT SUMMARY: Due to ethical violations, the Hendrys (P) sought return of fees they had paid attorney Pelland (D) despite a failure to prove causation between the alleged breaches and damages.

🏛 RULE OF LAW
Clients seeking disgorgement of legal fees as their sole remedy for a lawyer's breach of the duty of loyalty need prove only that their attorney breached that duty, not that the breach caused them injury.

FACTS: Pelland (D) represented the Hendrys (P) in a real estate transaction. The transaction proved unprofitable, and the Hendrys (P) sued Pelland (D) for alleged breach of ethical duties, seeking both damages and return of attorney fees. The district court held that Pelland (D) had violated conflict of interest rules. However, the court also held that, for fees to be disgorged, causation between the ethical violations and damages had to be proved. The Hendrys (P) appealed.

ISSUE: Do clients who are seeking disgorgement of legal fees as their sole remedy for a lawyer's breach of the duty of loyalty need prove only that their attorney breached that duty?

HOLDING AND DECISION: (Tatel, J.) Yes. Clients seeking disgorgement of legal fees as their sole remedy for a lawyer's breach of the duty of loyalty need prove only that their attorney breached that duty, not that the breach caused them injury. While normal rules of causation apply to compensatory damages awarded for professional negligence, this is not true for forfeiture of attorney fees. Public policy dictates that an attorney should not profit by unethical behavior. Therefore, any fees earned by an attorney in a representation that breaches his ethical duties are subject to forfeiture, even if the breach did not proximately cause any damages to the client. Here, the district court imposed a proximate cause requirement, and this was improper. Reversed.

▶ ANALYSIS

Courts differ as to the timing of disgorgement. Some hold that all fees earned in the representation must be forfeited. Others hold that only postbreach fees must be returned. Still others eschew a strict rule in this regard, and look to the circumstances of the case.

Quicknotes

DUTY OF LOYALTY A director's duty to refrain from self-dealing or to take a position that is adverse to the corporation's best interests.

FIDUCIARY DUTY A legal obligation to act for the benefit of another, including subordinating one's personal interests to that of the other person.

FORFEITURE The loss of a right or interest as a penalty for failing to fulfill an obligation.

Viner v. Sweet

Clients of attorney (P) v. Attorney (D)

Cal. Sup. Ct., 30 Cal. 4th 1232, 70 P.3d 1046 (2003).

NATURE OF CASE: Appeal from a damages award.

FACT SUMMARY: When the Viners (P) brought a malpractice action against their attorney, Sweet (D), for failure to properly prepare legal documents that would have protected the Viners (P), Sweet (D) argued that the plaintiff, in order to prevail in a transactional legal malpractice action, must prove that a more favorable result would have been obtained but for the alleged negligence.

🏛 RULE OF LAW
The plaintiff in a transactional legal malpractice action must prove that a more favorable result would have been obtained but for the alleged negligence.

FACTS: Michael and Deborah Viner (P) retained attorney Sweet (D) to draft various legal instruments in regard to their company, such as a securities purchase agreement and an employment termination agreement, which contained a noncompetition provision. In fact, the contracts failed to provide a variety of safeguards, which Sweet (D) had led the Viners (P) to believe were provided. Subsequently, disputes arose between the Viners (P) and companies with which they had contracted. Because the agreements failed to provide the protections that Sweet (D) had said were provided to the Viners (P), the Viners (P) alleged a large loss of income and consequently brought a malpractice action against Sweet (D). The jury awarded damages. The court of appeals reduced the damages award, but otherwise affirmed the judgment, stating that the "but for" test was inappropriate in a transactional legal malpractice action. Sweet (D) appealed, arguing that there is nothing distinctive about transactional malpractice to justify a relaxation of, or departure from, the well-established requirement in negligence cases that causation be established by the "but for" test.

ISSUE: Must the plaintiff in a transactional legal malpractice action prove that a more favorable result would have been obtained but for the alleged negligence?

HOLDING AND DECISION: (Kennard, J.) Yes. The plaintiff in a transactional legal malpractice action must prove that a more favorable result would have been obtained but for the alleged negligence. There is nothing distinctive about transactional malpractice to justify a relaxation of, or departure from, the well-established requirement in negligence cases that causation be established by the "but for" test. When a business transaction goes awry, a natural target of the disappointed principals is the attorneys who arranged or advised the deal. Clients predictably attempt to shift some part of the loss and disappointment of a deal that goes sour onto the shoulders of persons who were responsible for the underlying legal work. Before the loss can be shifted, however, the client has an initial hurdle to clear. It must be shown that the loss suffered was in fact caused by the alleged attorney malpractice. It is far too easy to make the legal advisor a scapegoat for a variety of business misjudgments unless the courts pay close attention to the cause in fact element, and deny recovery where the unfavorable outcome was likely to occur anyway, the client already knew the problems with the deal, or where the client's own misconduct or misjudgment caused the problems. It is the failure of the client to establish the causal link that explains decisions where the loss is termed remote or speculative. Courts are properly cautious about making attorneys guarantors of their clients' faulty business judgment. We do not agree with the court of appeals that litigation is inherently or necessarily less complex than transactional work. Some litigation, such as many lawsuits involving car accidents, is relatively uncomplicated, but so too is much transactional work, such as the negotiation of a simple lease or a purchase and sale agreement. But some litigation, such as a beneficiary's action against a trustee challenging the trustee's management of trust property over a period of decades, is as complex as most transactional work. Furthermore, an attorney's representation of a client often combines litigation and transactional work, as when the attorney effects a settlement of pending litigation. Reversed.

▶ ANALYSIS

As the California Supreme Court points out in the *Viner* decision, the purpose of the "but for" requirement, which has been in use for more than 120 years, is to safeguard against speculative and conjectural claims. It serves the essential purpose of ensuring that damages awarded for the attorney's malpractice "actually have been caused by the malpractice."

■=■

Quicknotes

FIDUCIARY DUTY A legal obligation to act for the benefit of another, including subordinating one's personal interests to that of the other person.

PROFESSIONAL NEGLIGENCE The breach of a fiduciary duty owed to one's client, caused by the professional's actions and injurious to the client.

■=■

Peeler v. Hughes & Luce

Corporate officer (P) v. Law firm (D)

Tex. Sup. Ct., 909 S.W.2d 494 (Tex. 1995).

NATURE OF CASE: Appeal from dismissal of malpractice action.

FACT SUMMARY: Peeler (P), who had accepted a plea bargain in a prosecution in which she had been defended by Hughes & Luce (D), sued the firm for malpractice when she learned that a prosecutorial offer of immunity had not been communicated to her.

🏛 RULE OF LAW
A legal malpractice claim may not be brought in the context of a criminal matter absent a showing that the plaintiff has been exonerated from the conviction.

FACTS: Peeler (P) and her husband were indicted on numerous counts of tax-related crimes. She eventually accepted a plea bargain in which all but one of the charges against her were dropped, resulting in a short sentence and a fine. Subsequent to pleading guilty, she discovered that the prosecutor had conveyed to her attorney at Hughes & Luce (D) an offer of absolute transactional immunity in exchange for testifying against alleged co-conspirators. This offer had never been communicated to her. She sued Hughes & Luce (D) for malpractice. The trial court granted Hughes & Luce's (D) motion for summary judgment, dismissing the action. The court of appeals affirmed, and the state supreme court granted review.

ISSUE: May a legal malpractice claim be brought in the context of a criminal matter absent a showing that the plaintiff has been exonerated from the conviction?

HOLDING AND DECISION: (Enoch, J.) No. A legal malpractice claim may not be brought in the context of a criminal matter absent a showing that the plaintiff has been exonerated from the conviction. This is because criminal conduct is the only cause of any injury suffered as a result of conviction. Therefore only innocent plaintiffs can negate the sole-proximate-cause bar to their cause of action for professional negligence. Thus a criminal defendant who has been found guilty, either by plea or verdict, cannot sue his attorneys for malpractice unless the conviction is later overturned on direct appeal or collateral attack. To hold otherwise would allow the criminal to financially profit from his misdeed, something the law cannot countenance. In this instance, Peeler (P) was convicted through a guilty plea and never even asserted that she did not commit the acts for which she was indicted, so she has no action against Hughes & Luce (D). Affirmed.

CONCURRENCE: (Hightower, J.) The holding today should not be read as condoning the alleged malfeasance of Peeler's (P) attorney which, if true, was reprehensible and unconscionable.

DISSENT: (Phillips, C.J.) An exception to the rule cited by the court should be made when it can be shown that, but for the alleged malpractice, the defendant would not have been convicted.

▶ ANALYSIS

The rule cited here leaves a hapless convict with something of a Catch-22: If his attorney's malpractice lands him in prison, he has no recourse against the attorney. The only hope for one in a position such as Peeler (P) found herself would be an appeal or habeas proceeding based on ineffective counsel in violation of the Sixth Amendment. However, even this remedy is probably unavailable to one who plea bargains.

∎≡∎

Quicknotes

PROFESSIONAL NEGLIGENCE The breach of a fiduciary duty owed to one's client, caused by the professional's actions and injurious to the client.

PROXIMATE CAUSE The natural sequence of events without which an injury would not have been sustained.

TRANSACTIONAL IMMUNITY Also called the privilege against self-incrimination; a person's constitutional right to refuse to render testimony that may incriminate them if called as a witness.

∎≡∎

Petrillo v. Bachenberg

Land purchaser (P) v. Real estate broker (D)

N.J. Sup. Ct., 139 N.J. 472, 655 A.2d 1354 (1995).

NATURE OF CASE: Review of order reversing dismissal of negligent misrepresentation claim.

FACT SUMMARY: Petrillo (P) sued attorney Herrigel (D) for preparation of a misleading composite report even though Herrigel (D) had never represented her.

🏛 RULE OF LAW
Attorneys may owe a duty of care to nonclients when the attorneys know, or should know, that nonclients will rely on the attorneys' representations and the nonclients are not too remote from the attorneys to be entitled to protection.

FACTS: Developer Rohrer Construction and its attorney, Herrigel (D), solicited from a soils engineer tests regarding the suitability of certain real estate for the placement of a septic system. Two series of tests were performed that indicated that the land was unsuitable. A report was compiled from the two series of tests that gave the impression that the land was in fact suitable. The land was eventually purchased at a foreclosure sale by Bachenberg (D), who then retained Herrigel (D), who passed on to him the erroneous report. The land was then sold to Petrillo (P) for commercial development. Petrillo (P), who had been given a copy of the report during her negotiations to purchase the property, hired an engineering firm to conduct her own tests, which showed that the land could not be brought into compliance with local ordinances and was undevelopable. She then sued Bachenberg (D) for return of the purchase money, and Herrigel (D) for providing the erroneous report. The trial court dismissed the claim against Herrigel (D), but the court of appeals reversed. The state supreme court granted review.

ISSUE: May attorneys owe a duty of care to nonclients?

HOLDING AND DECISION: (Pollock, J.) Yes. Attorneys may owe a duty of care to nonclients when the attorneys know, or should know, that nonclients will rely on the attorneys' representations and the nonclients are not too remote from the attorneys to be entitled to protection. At common law, an attorney was not liable to a nonclient due to lack of privity. This rule has slowly been replaced with one that looks more to the overall circumstances to ascertain whether the attorney should have liability imposed on him for injury to a nonclient. Generally speaking, if a lawyer negligently prepares a document and such document is foreseeably to be used by third parties, such parties have recourse against the attorney. Examples of such situations include opinion letters and securities offering statements. Here, it was foreseeable that a purchaser of the property

would rely on the soils report in making a purchase decision, so Herrigel's (D) duty extended to Petrillo (P). A jury should have the opportunity to decide the effect of Herrigel's (D) alleged negligent misrepresentation. Affirmed.

CONCURRENCE: (Stein, J.) The current decision effects no material change in the law in this area.

DISSENT: (Garibaldi, J.) As Petrillo (P) did not rely on any opinion offered by Herriger (D), he owed no duty of care to her.

▶ ANALYSIS

The Washington Supreme Court has formulated a balancing test to determine when lawyers may be held liable to nonclients. Factors to be considered include the extent to which the transaction was intended to benefit the plaintiff, the foreseeability of harm to the plaintiff, and the closeness of the connection between the defendant's conduct and the injury. Policy considerations include prevention of future harm and the extent to which the legal profession would be unduly burdened by a finding of liability. See *Trask v. Butler*, 872 P.2d 1080 (1994).

Quicknotes

DUTY OF CARE A principle of negligence requiring an individual to act in such a manner as to avoid injury to a person to whom he or she owes an obligatory duty.

PRIVITY Commonality of rights or interests between parties.

In re Warhaftig

n/a

N.J. Sup. Ct., 106 N.J. 529, 524 A.2d 398 (1987).

NATURE OF CASE: Attorney disciplinary proceeding.

FACT SUMMARY: Warhaftig (D) appropriated client funds, although he did so with the intention of repaying the funds.

🏛 RULE OF LAW
An attorney may be disbarred for taking fee advances out of client funds, even if he did so with the intention of returning the funds.

FACTS: Attorney Warhaftig (D), faced with serious financial pressures, began appropriating client funds. For the most part, the funds were returned. When the State Bar (P) discovered Warhaftig's (D) activities, it instituted disciplinary proceedings. Warhaftig (D) argued in his defense that he had only meant to "borrow" the monies taken, not permanently misappropriate them. Based on this distinction, the State Bar (P) recommended a reprimand but not disbarment. The state supreme court reviewed the conclusions.

ISSUE: May an attorney be disbarred for taking fee advances out of client funds, even if he did so with the intention of returning the funds?

HOLDING AND DECISION: (Per curiam) Yes. An attorney may be disbarred for taking fee advances out of client funds, even if he did so with the intention of returning the funds. This court has ruled that an attorney who knowingly misappropriates client funds must be disbarred. The distinction made by the State Bar (P) in this instance is misplaced. Misappropriation is prohibited, whether or not the funds are "stolen" or "borrowed." A bank teller can hardly use this excuse if his employer finds him taking funds, and an attorney should be held to at least as high a standard. Here, Warhaftig (D) knowingly took funds to which he was not entitled, and this ends the inquiry. [The court then held mitigating factors to be insufficient, and ordered Warhaftig (D) disbarred.]

▶ ANALYSIS

The court did admit that Warhaftig (D) may not have been as culpable as if he had had no intent to repay his client's money, but the court found the difference to be only negligible. Of course, to trigger automatic disbarment, the misappropriation must be "knowing." Merely careless bookkeeping or accidental use of client monies will not subject an attorney to disbarment, but may result in sanctions for failure to protect client property.

Quicknotes

DISBARMENT The administrative penalty levied against an attorney for a breach of professional conduct that effectively revokes the license to practice law.

MISAPPROPRIATION The unlawful use of another's property or funds.

■■■

In re Austern

n/a

D.C. Ct. App., 524 A.2d 680 (1987).

NATURE OF CASE: Review of recommendation of public censure.

FACT SUMMARY: Austern was recommended for censure for facilitating a real estate transaction despite knowledge that his client's deposit into an escrow account was a check drawn from nonexistent funds.

🏛 RULE OF LAW
An attorney may be censured for facilitating a real estate transaction despite knowledge that a client's deposit to third parties consisted of a check drawn on nonexistent funds.

FACTS: Austern represented one Viorst, who was attempting to arrange a condominium conversion. At one point he attended a meeting between Viorst and prospective purchasers. The purchasers, suspicious of Viorst's motives, demanded that he make a good faith money deposit into an escrow account. Viorst wrote a check for $10,000. Viorst later admitted to Austern that the check was drawn on an account which contained no funds. Despite this knowledge, Austern helped effect the transaction. He was later investigated by the Board on Professional Responsibility, which recommended censure for his part in the deal. The court of appeals for the jurisdiction, the District of Columbia, renewed the recommendation.

ISSUE: May an attorney be censured for facilitating a real estate transaction despite knowledge that a client's deposit to third parties consisted of a check drawn on nonexistent funds?

HOLDING AND DECISION: (Pryor, C.J.) Yes. An attorney may be censured for facilitating a real estate transaction despite knowledge that a client's deposit to third parties consisted of a check drawn on nonexistent funds. DR 1 102(A)(4) and DR 7-102(A)(7) provide that an attorney will not further an illegal or fraudulent purpose. Here, Viorst's use of a worthless check as earnest money constituted a fraud on the prospective purchasers. Austern, with knowledge of this fraud, helped facilitate the transaction. This was a clear violation of DR 1-102(A)(4) and DR 7-102(A)(7). The only appropriate course of action for Austern would have been to advise Viorst to cease and, upon Viorst's failure to do so, withdraw. His failure to do so was censurable. Affirmed.

▶ ANALYSIS

An attorney is permitted to represent a client who has already engaged in illegal or fraudulent conduct. However, an attorney cannot represent a client whom one knows to be engaging in ongoing illegal or fraudulent conduct. All jurisdictions have rules identical to or similar to those invoked here. Austern's conduct would have been censurable almost anywhere.

■══■

Quicknotes

CENSURE A statement issued by a governing body toward one of its members officially reprimanding that person.

DR 7-102 (A)(7) A client is not entitled to affirmative assistance by his attorney in conduct that the lawyer knows to be illegal or fraudulent. If an attorney is faced with such a situation he is under an affirmative duty to withdraw from representation.

■══■

Matter of Tsoutsouris

n/a

Ind. Sup. Ct., 748 N.E.2d 856 (2001).

NATURE OF CASE: Appeal from judgment suspending a lawyer from practice.

FACT SUMMARY: An attorney was suspended from the practice of law for thirty days for having a sexual relationship with a client while representing her.

🏛 RULE OF LAW
It is professional misconduct for a lawyer to engage in sexual relations with a current client, unless the relationship commenced before representation.

FACTS: The respondent, an attorney, engaged in a sexual relationship with his client, a woman who was obtaining a divorce, during the course of their professional relationship. The attorney failed to inform his client how the sexual relationship might affect his professional responsibilities to her or their attorney-client relationship. The attorney ended the affair a few weeks after it began. Two years later, the client again hired the attorney for another matter and later sought psychological treatment relating to her relationship with the attorney.

ISSUE: Is it professional misconduct for a lawyer to engage in a sexual relationship with a current client?

HOLDING AND DECISION: (Per curiam) Yes. A lawyer may not represent a client if the representation is materially limited by the lawyer's own interests. A lawyer's ability to effectively represent a client may be impaired when the lawyer is having sexual relations with that client. His or her independent professional judgment may be hindered, or the ability to remain objectively detached could be lost. However, the court found no evidence that the client's legal position was harmed in any way, particularly because the client hired the attorney to perform another legal service for her after the sexual relationship was over. The court suspended the respondent from the practice of law for thirty days in light of this mitigating factor and his thirty-three year record of discipline-free practice. Affirmed.

▶ *ANALYSIS*

Clients often place enormous trust in their lawyers, particularly criminal defendants and matrimonial clients. Lawyers, therefore, have a responsibility to preserve and protect that trust, as well as effectively to represent their clients. By engaging in sexual relations with a client who may be in a particularly vulnerable state, the attorney breaches that fiduciary responsibility. It is a better practice to refrain from becoming sexually intimate with a client during the course of that representation.

■═■

Quicknotes

MISCONDUCT Conduct that is unlawful or otherwise improper.

■═■

Matter of Jordan Schiff

n/a

Departmental Disciplinary Committee, N.Y. Sup. Ct., Docket No. HP 22/92 (1993).

NATURE OF CASE: Disciplinary action taken in response to allegations of misconduct by an attorney during a deposition.

FACT SUMMARY: This disciplinary hearing was held after Schiff (D) allegedly violated the code of ethics by using obscene, explicit, gender-specific vulgarities to harass opposing female counsel during a deposition.

🏛 RULE OF LAW
Attorneys who direct dirty, discriminatory, gutter language at opposing counsel to harass counsel on the basis of gender will be subject to sanction for violation of the rules of professional ethics.

FACTS: During a deposition of a client which his firm represented in a personal injury suit, Schiff (D) used obscene, explicit, gender-specific vulgarities in an attempt to intimidate and harass opposing counsel, Mark (P). Early in the deposition, a senior partner of Schiff's (D) firm had set the tone by standing and shouting at Mark (P). During a hearing held by the Disciplinary Committee, both the court reporter and the Spanish interpreter testified that, off the record, Schiff (D) referred to Mark (P) as a "cunt" and an "asshole" and said she should "go home and have babies." On the record, the deposition itself was replete with sexual obscenities uttered by Schiff (D).

ISSUE: Will attorneys who direct dirty, discriminatory, gutter language at opposing counsel to harass counsel on the basis of gender be subject to sanction for violation of the rules of professional ethics?

HOLDING AND DECISION: (Elsen, Panel Chair) Yes. Attorneys who direct dirty, discriminatory, gutter language at opposing counsel to harass counsel on the basis of gender will be subject to sanction for violation of the rules of professional ethics. In mitigation, Schiff (D) apologized to Mark (P) by letter and at the hearing. However, the record shows that the apology and sanctions imposed on Schiff's (D) law firm were insufficient to convince him that his conduct was in need of reform. Evidence of a later deposition in another case reveals Schiff (D) used gender-specific vulgarities again in speaking to opposing female counsel. On the evidence presented, all charges against Schiff (D) of ethics violations are sustained. The sanction will be public censure.

▶ ANALYSIS

The panel declared that were it not for Schiff's (D) unblemished record and his youth, plus the consideration that he was no longer with the firm that set him such a bad example,

their recommendation would be even more severe. Public censure was deemed appropriate because those in the profession must understand that sexual harassment is unacceptable, and the public must understand that the profession abhors such behavior and will not condone it. In censuring Schiff (D), *Matter of Schiff*, 190 A.D.2d 293 (1993), the court described his conduct as "inexcusable and intolerable, reflecting adversely on his fitness to practice law."

Quicknotes

PUBLIC CENSURE A statement issued by a governing body toward one of its members officially reprimanding that person, and carrying a higher degree of professional disgrace than a simple reprimand because it is made public.

Strickland v. Washington

Convicted murderer (D) v. State of Washington (P)

466 U.S. 668 (1984).

NATURE OF CASE: Review of death sentence imposed subsequent to murder conviction.

FACT SUMMARY: Strickland (D) challenged his death sentence on the ground that the lawyer who represented him at the hearing was constitutionally ineffective.

🏛 RULE OF LAW
A court deciding on ineffectiveness of counsel claim at a death sentence hearing must judge whether counsel's conduct was reasonable under the facts as viewed at the time of the alleged ineffectiveness.

FACTS: Strickland (D) was charged and convicted of murder. Per Washington law, a hearing was held as to the appropriate sentence. Strickland (D) was sentenced to death. He petitioned for certiorari to the U.S. Supreme Court, contending that he was denied effective assistance of counsel in violation of the Sixth Amendment. [The casebook excerpt did not state the basis for Strickland's (D) claim.]

ISSUE: Must a court deciding an ineffectiveness of counsel claim at a death sentence hearing judge whether counsel's conduct was reasonable as viewed at the time of the alleged ineffectiveness?

HOLDING AND DECISION: (O'Connor, J.) Yes. A court deciding an ineffectiveness of counsel claim at a death sentence hearing must judge whether counsel's conduct was reasonable as viewed at the time of the alleged ineffectiveness, and the defendant, having shown such ineffectiveness, must demonstrate a reasonable probability that the outcome would have been different but for the mistake. Since a death sentence hearing is an adversarial process not unlike a trial, the standard for a claim of constitutional ineffectiveness at the hearing is like that for trial: the defendant must show that counsel made errors so serious that counsel was not functioning as "counsel." Secondly, the defendant must show that the deficient performance so prejudiced the defense as to deprive the defendant of a fair trial. The proper standard for attorney performance is that of reasonably effective assistance, and what is "reasonable" must be viewed in light of what counsel knew or should have known at the time of trial. Courts should not indulge in hindsight or second-guessing of counsel lightly; it is presumed that counsel fulfilled its duty of loyalty and competence. To hold that courts can at-will scrutinize performance of counsel would encourage proliferation of ineffectiveness challenges. Therefore, only if a court can say that counsel definitely committed errors which should not have been made considering that which it knew or should have known at the time of the errors will counsel be considered ineffective. As to the prejudice requirement, it is not enough to show the mere possibility of prejudice. Such possibility will always exist, and more is required to show constitutional error. Rather, a defendant must show that confidence in the outcome has been undermined. This Court believes that the proper standard is that it be reasonably probable that the ineffectiveness altered the outcome of the proceeding. [The casebook excerpt omitted analysis of the facts of the case to the standard described herein.]

▶ ANALYSIS

Rule 8.6(a) of the ABA standards relating to the Defense Function provides: "If a lawyer, after investigation, is satisfied that another lawyer who served in an earlier phase of the case did not provide effective assistance, he should not hesitate to seek relief for the defendant on that ground." This would seem to provide an invitation for ineffectiveness challenges. However, as the present opinion makes clear, the Court is not disposed toward such challenges.

■=■

Quicknotes

CERTIORARI A discretionary writ issued by a superior court to an inferior court in order to review the lower court's decisions; the Supreme Court's writ ordering such review.

INEFFECTIVE ASSISTANCE OF COUNSEL A claim brought by an accused in which it must be determined whether the attorney's rendering of representation was such that the ultimate disposition of the case may not be relied upon as fair.

■=■

United States v. Cronic

Federal government (P) v. Mail fraud convict (D)

466 U.S. 648 (1984).

NATURE OF CASE: Appeal from reversal of a conviction for mail fraud on the ground of ineffective assistance of counsel.

FACT SUMMARY: After Cronic (D) was tried and convicted on charges of mail fraud, the court of appeals reversed on the ground that Cronic (D) had received ineffective assistance of counsel.

🏛 RULE OF LAW
A defendant can make out a claim of ineffective assistance only by pointing to specific errors made by trial counsel unless surrounding circumstances justify a presumption of ineffectiveness.

FACTS: Cronic (D) was charged with mail fraud. At the time counsel was appointed to represent Cronic (D), the trial was to begin eighteen days later. Counsel requested a thirty-day continuance. However, the court granted only a twenty-five-day continuance. After Cronic (D) received a twenty-five-year sentence on the mail fraud charge, the court of appeals, purportedly applying a standard of reasonable competence, reversed Cronic's (D) conviction on the ground of ineffective assistance of counsel. The United States (P) appealed, and the Supreme Court granted certiorari.

ISSUE: May a defendant make out a claim of ineffective assistance of counsel only by pointing to specific errors made by trial counsel?

HOLDING AND DECISION: (Stevens, J.) Yes. A defendant may make out a claim of ineffective assistance of counsel only by pointing to specific errors made by trial counsel. The right to the effective assistance of counsel is the right of the accused to require the prosecution's case to survive the crucible of meaningful adversarial testing. When a true adversarial criminal trial has been conducted, even if defense counsel may have made demonstrable errors, the kind of testing envisioned by the Sixth Amendment has occurred. This case is not one in which the surrounding circumstances make it unlikely that Cronic (D) could have received the effective assistance of counsel. He can thus make out a claim of ineffective assistance only by pointing to specific errors made by trial counsel. Remanded to give Cronic (D) an opportunity to demonstrate such specific errors.

▶ ANALYSIS

Finding specific errors on remand, *United States v. Cronic*, 839 F.2d 1401 (10th Cir. 1988), the Tenth Circuit vacated the conviction, ordering a new trial. In general, courts are highly deferential to strategies devised by lawyers. As long as the lawyer carries through the devised strategy, he or she will rarely be found wanting, even when the strategy fails. Such errors of commission are generally left to malpractice suits.

■══■

Quicknotes

INEFFECTIVE ASSISTANCE OF COUNSEL A claim brought by an accused in which it must be determined whether the attorney's rendering of representation was such that the ultimate disposition of the case may not be relied upon as fair.

■══■

CHAPTER 14

Control of Quality: Lay Participation in Law Business

Quick Reference Rules of Law

NAACP v. Button

Political organization (P) v. State official (D)

371 U.S. 415 (1963).

NATURE OF CASE: Review of order rejecting constitutional challenge to anti-solicitation law.

FACT SUMMARY: Virginia (D) enacted a law prohibiting the solicitation of clients by an agent of an organization or individual that retained a lawyer in connection with an action in which it was neither a party nor had a pecuniary interest.

RULE OF LAW
A state may not constitutionally prohibit the solicitation of clients by an agent of an individual or organization that retains a lawyer in connection with an action in which it is neither a party nor has a pecuniary interest.

FACTS: The Virginia Chapter of the National Association for the Advancement of Colored People (the NAACP) (P) had for years engaged in the activity of locating (soliciting) potential plaintiffs to be litigants in suits aimed at fulfilling the NAACP's (P) political objectives of ending segregation. In response, the state of Virginia (D) enacted an anti-solicitation law prohibiting the agent of an organization or individual from soliciting clients for lawsuits in which the organization or individual paid for the lawyer in connection with an action in which the organization or individual was neither a party nor had a pecuniary interest. As the attorneys to whom the NAACP (P) would refer potential litigants were usually on the NAACP (P) staff, this effectively prohibited the NAACP's (P) solicitation procedure. The NAACP (P) challenged this as violative of the First Amendment. The state's highest court rejected this contention, and the U.S. Supreme Court granted certiorari.

ISSUE: May a state constitutionally prohibit the solicitation of clients by an agent of an individual or organization that retains a lawyer in connection with an action in which it is neither a party nor has a pecuniary interest?

HOLDING AND DECISION: (Brennan, J.) No. A state may not constitutionally prohibit the solicitation of clients by an agent of an individual or organization that retains a lawyer in connection with an action in which it is neither a party nor has a pecuniary interest. Solicitation is covered by the First Amendment, since abstract discussion is not the only species of communication protected by the First Amendment; vigorous advocacy is protected by it as well. Litigation is more than a vehicle for resolving private disputes; it is a means for achieving lawful political ends, and in that regard it is political expression. Under the conditions of government, litigation is sometimes the only practicable way an unpopular group can petition for redress of grievances. The First Amendment protects certain forms of group activity, and using litigation to achieve political ends is one such form of activity. That is, association for litigation is a form of political association. Under the statute at issue, a person who advises another that his legal rights have been infringed and refers him to a particular attorney or group of attorneys for assistance has committed a crime, as has the attorney who knowingly renders assistance under such circumstances; the statute thus poses the grave danger of unconstitutionally eliminating any discussion relating to the institution of litigation on behalf of unpopular minorities. Since the use of litigation is a constitutionally protected activity, Virginia (D) must show a compelling reason for its existence. The proffered justification is the state interest in regulating the legal profession and against solicitation and barratry. While these are important objectives, the type of solicitation at issue here differs materially from solicitation of a for-profit nature, which a state may well be able to prohibit. Such is not at issue here. Since a compelling reason for the prohibition has not been shown, it is constitutionally defective. Reversed.

DISSENT: (Harlan, J.) An attorney retained by the NAACP (P) to promote its causes—ordinarily an NAACP (P) staff attorney—does not form a normal attorney-client relationship with his "client." The form of pleading, the relief requested, and the timing of lawsuits are all decided by the NAACP (P), not the attorney, to whom he is essentially beholden. Virginia (D) has an interest in maintaining high professional standards in its legal profession. It has never been seriously disputed that laws against solicitation and barratry are valid, and the law at issue finds its roots therein. The majority distinguishes the statute from other types of regulation of solicitation and barratry by noting that the type of suits the NAACP (P) initiates are not of the for-profit nature. This is a too-facile analysis, since the avoidance of pecuniary gain is not the only relevant factor in determining appropriate standards of lawyer conduct. A lawyer in the type of actions maintained by the NAACP (P) finds himself in a divided allegiance. A state has an interest in preventing attorney conflicts of interest, and this legitimizes the law in question. Moreover, the statute here does not unreasonably impede the assertion of federal rights and is consistent with federal standing rules.

► ANALYSIS

Ethical Consideration 5-1 of Canon 5 of the ABA Code of Professional Responsibility provides: "The professional judgment of a lawyer should be exercised, within the bounds of

Continued on next page.

the law, solely for the benefit of his client and free of compromising influences and loyalties. Neither his personal interests, the interests of other clients, nor the desires of third persons should be permitted to dilute his loyalty to his client." An attorney retained by an organization which has solicited litigants to further its political ends through litigation will almost certainly have to deal with this consideration at some point, and may at some point face a conflict of interest that will require the attorney's withdrawal.

■══■

Quicknotes

CONFLICT OF INTEREST Refers to ethical problems that arise, or may be anticipated to arise, between an attorney and his client if the interests of the attorney, another client or a third party conflict with those of the present client.

RETAINER Compensation paid in advance for professional services.

■══■

United Transportation Union v. State Bar of Michigan

Railworkers' union (D) v. Michigan state bar (P)

401 U.S. 576 (1971).

NATURE OF CASE: Review of order enjoining a labor union from procuring legal services for its members.

FACT SUMMARY: The Michigan State Bar (P) challenged the United Transportation Union's (D) practice of obtaining low-cost legal services for its members.

🏛 RULE OF LAW
A labor union can assist its members in obtaining low-cost legal services.

FACTS: The United Transportation Union (D) instituted a program to assist its members who had causes of action under the Federal Employers' Liability Act. The Union (D) would refer its members to selected attorneys, who had agreed to charge a fee of no more than 25% of total recovery. The Michigan State Bar (P) challenged this practice as illegal "solicitation" of lawsuits. A state trial court enjoined the practice, and the Michigan Supreme Court affirmed. The U.S. Supreme Court granted review.

ISSUE: Can a labor union assist its members in obtaining low-cost legal services?

HOLDING AND DECISION: (Black, J.) Yes. A labor union can assist its members in obtaining low-cost legal services. This Court has already held that the First Amendment permits groups to unite to assert their legal rights as effectively and economically as possible. An organization may also employ attorneys to represent its members. From this it follows that an organization may also refer its members to attorneys. The injunction at issue here not only prohibited the Union (D) from so doing, but also enjoined it from doing various acts incident thereto, such as providing information concerning the availability of legal service and compensating individuals for the time spent providing such information. If an organization is to be permitted to assert its legal rights, the activities enjoined in this particular case must also be permitted. Reversed.

▶ ANALYSIS

The case principally relied upon by the Court here was *NAACP v. Button*, 371 U.S. 415 (1963). A difference existed between the situation in *NAACP* and the present case, in that the prior action involved ideologically motivated litigation as opposed to the purely economic interests at issue here. It is not clear whether this distinction was raised, and based on the Court's inclinations as evidenced by the language of the opinion, it is unlikely that it would have altered the holding.

Quicknotes

FIRST AMENDMENT Prohibits Congress from enacting any law respecting an establishment of religion, prohibiting the free exercise of religion, abridging freedom of speech or the press, the right of peaceful assembly and the right to petition for a redress of grievances.

■━■

CHAPTER **15**

Free Speech Rights of Lawyers and Judicial Candidates

Quick Reference Rules of Law

1. **Public Comment About Pending Cases.** Public utterances by an attorney need not present a clear and present danger to a fair trial to be subject to prohibition. (Gentile v. State Bar of Nevada) *98*

2. **Public Comment About Judges and Courts.** It is not necessary for an attorney to act with constitutional malice in order for the attorney to be disciplined for issuing false statements. (Matter of Holtzman) *99*

3. **Judicial Campaign Speech.** The First Amendment prohibits a state's judiciary from prohibiting candidates for judicial election in that state from announcing their views on disputed legal and political issues. (Republican Party of Minnesota v. White) *100*

97

Gentile v. State Bar of Nevada

Criminal defense attorney (D) v. Nevada state bar (P)

501 U.S. 1030 (1991).

NATURE OF CASE: Review of attorney disciplinary order of reprimand.

FACT SUMMARY: Gentile (D), reprimanded for speaking to the press about a pending prosecution, contended that such speech could only be prohibited when it constituted a clear and present danger to a fair trial.

🏛 RULE OF LAW
Public utterances by an attorney need not present a clear and present danger to a fair trial to be subject to prohibition.

FACTS: Gentile (D), a Nevada attorney, undertook to represent one Sanders, who had been indicted for theft. Six months prior to trial, he held a press conference wherein he made certain charges of a cover-up by local police and prosecutors. He was later reprimanded by the State Bar (P) for violating Nevada Supreme Court Rule 177, which prohibited an attorney from speaking about a pending case if such speech had a substantial likelihood of influencing the outcome of the case. He petitioned for certiorari, contending that, consistent with the First Amendment, only speech showing a clear and present danger of denying a fair trial could be prohibited.

ISSUE: Must public utterances by an attorney present a clear and present danger to a fair trial to be subject to prohibition?

HOLDING AND DECISION: (Rehnquist, C.J.) No. Public utterances by an attorney need not present a clear and present danger to a fair trial to be subject to prohibition. An attorney does not park his free speech rights at the courthouse door. Nonetheless, the governmental interest in ensuring fair trials exerts sufficient influence on an attorney's role that, to the extent an attorney's speech might tend to have improper influence on a case, that speech may be regulated under a standard less demanding than that of "clear and present danger." The standard employed here, that of "substantial likelihood of material prejudice," has been adopted by a majority of states, and this Court agrees that it represents a proper balancing of an attorney's free speech rights with the state's interest in a fair trial, and hereby adopts it as the appropriate standard in this area. [In a separate opinion by Justice Kennedy, joined by four other justices and therefore constituting a majority opinion, it was held that Rule 177's "safe haven" provisions were constitutionally void for vagueness, and the reprimand was reversed on these grounds.]

CONCURRENCE: (O'Connor, J.) Gentile (D) seemed to have stayed within Rule 177's safe haven provisions and the State Bar's (P) view that he did not underscores its vagueness.

▶ ANALYSIS

Attorney freedom of speech issues usually arise in the context of advertising, a form of commercial speech. The impact of the First Amendment on commercial speech is somewhat different to that involved here. The analysis used here is not necessarily applicable to advertising cases.

■■■

Quicknotes

NEVADA SUPREME COURT RULE 177 Prohibits the dissemination of information that an attorney knows or reasonably should know has a substantial likelihood of materially prejudicing an adjudicative proceeding.

■■■

Matter of Holtzman

n/a

N.Y. Ct. App., 78 N.Y.2d 184, 577 N.E.2d 30, 573 N.Y.S.2d 39, *cert. denied*, 502 U.S. 1009 (1991).

NATURE OF CASE: Appeal of admonition for attorney conduct.

FACT SUMMARY: Holtzman (D), admonished for falsely accusing a judge of improper behavior, contended that such an admonition required a finding of constitutional malice.

🏛 RULE OF LAW
It is not necessary for an attorney to act with constitutional malice in order for the attorney to be disciplined for issuing false statements.

FACTS: Holtzman (D), the Kings County District Attorney, released a letter to the media alleging that a trial court judge behaved improperly. An investigation revealed that her accusations were false. She was then admonished under attorney disciplinary rules for the false accusations. She appealed the admonition, contending that state bar authorities had to find that she acted with constitutional malice in order to discipline her.

ISSUE: Is it necessary for an attorney to act with constitutional malice in order for the attorney to be disciplined for issuing false statements?

HOLDING AND DECISION: (Per curiam) No. It is not necessary for an attorney to act with constitutional malice in order for the attorney to be disciplined for issuing false statements. Unlike defamation, to which constitutional malice applies, professional responsibility is not an essentially private matter but rather is rendered for the benefit of the public at large. When an attorney makes a false statement, the issue is not whether a reputation has been harmed but rather whether the administration of justice has been hampered. To substitute objective analysis of this question with the subjective standard of constitutional malice would undercut the premise of professional responsibility, which would be against the public interest. Affirmed.

▶ ANALYSIS

In the adversarial atmosphere of the courtroom, it is natural that attorneys and judges will lock horns. This sometimes results in public statements by attorneys about judges that are less than flattering. All states have limits on what attorneys can say about judges, limits which attorneys often cross to their regret.

Quicknotes

MALICE The intention to commit an unlawful act without justification or excuse.

NEW YORK CODE OF PROFESSIONAL RESPONSIBILITY DR 1-102 (A)(6) A lawyer shall not engage in any other conduct that adversely reflects on his fitness to practice law.

■═■

Republican Party of Minnesota v. White

Political party (P) v. State judicial official (D)

536 U.S. 765 (2002).

NATURE OF CASE: Appeal from decision that a state's judiciary, without violating the First Amendment, may prohibit candidates for judicial election in that state from announcing their views on disputed legal or political issues.

FACT SUMMARY: The state's highest court adopted a canon of judicial conduct that prohibited a candidate for judicial office from "announc[ing] his or her views on disputed legal or political issues" (announce clause). While running for associate justice of that court, Wersal (and others) (P) filed suit seeking a declaration that the announce clause violated the First Amendment.

🏛 RULE OF LAW
The First Amendment prohibits a state's judiciary from prohibiting candidates for judicial election in that state from announcing their views on disputed legal and political issues.

FACTS: The state's highest court adopted a canon of judicial conduct that prohibited a "candidate for a judicial office" from "announc[ing] his or her views on disputed legal or political issues" (announce clause). Incumbent judges who violated this rule were subject to discipline, including removal, censure, civil penalties, and suspension without pay. Lawyers who ran for judicial office also had to comply with the announce clause. While running for associate justice of the state's highest court, Wersal (and others) (P) filed suit in federal district court seeking a declaration that the announce clause was violative of the First Amendment and an injunction against its enforcement. The district court held that the announce clause was constitutional and granted summary judgment to the state (D). The court of appeals affirmed, and the United States Supreme Court granted certiorari.

ISSUE: Does the First Amendment prohibit a state's judiciary from prohibiting candidates for judicial election in that state from announcing their views on disputed legal and political issues?

HOLDING AND DECISION: (Scalia, J.) Yes. The First Amendment prohibits a state's judiciary from prohibiting candidates for judicial election in that state from announcing their views on disputed legal and political issues. "Announcing views" on an issue covers much more than promising to decide an issue a certain way, and the announce clause prohibits a candidate's mere statements of his current position, even if he doesn't bind himself to maintain that position after election. Although the clause was construed in the courts below to reach only disputed issues that are likely to come before the candidate if he is elected, this limitation is not much of a limitation because

there is almost no legal or political issue that is unlikely to come before a judge of an American court. The record demonstrates that the announce clause prohibits a judicial candidate from stating his views on any specific nonfanciful legal question within the province of the court for which he is running, except in the context of discussing past decisions—and in the latter context as well, if he expresses the view that he is not bound by stare decisis. The state (D) argues that this still leaves plenty of topics for discussion on the campaign trail, such as a candidate's character, education, work habits, etc., and, in fact, the state's (D) judicial board has published a list of preapproved questions that judicial candidates are allowed to answer. The issue then becomes whether these preapproved subjects fulfill the First Amendment's free speech guarantee. The announce clause both prohibits speech based on its content and burdens a category of speech that is at the core of First Amendment freedoms—speech about the qualifications of candidates for public office. The court of appeals concluded, and the parties do not dispute, that the proper test to be applied to determine the constitutionality of such a restriction is strict scrutiny, under which respondents have the burden to prove that the clause is (1) narrowly tailored, to serve (2) a compelling state interest. That court found that the state (D) had established two interests as sufficiently compelling to justify the announce clause: preserving the state judiciary's impartiality and preserving the appearance of that impartiality. Under any definition of "impartiality," the announce clause fails strict scrutiny. First, it is plain that the clause is not narrowly tailored to serve impartiality (or its appearance) in the traditional sense of the word, i.e., as a lack of bias for or against either party to the proceeding. Indeed, the clause is barely tailored to serve that interest at all, inasmuch as it does not restrict speech for or against particular parties, but rather speech for or against particular issues. If a party loses a case that turns on a legal issue the judge had taken a stand on as a candidate, it is not because of bias against the party, but because the judge is evenhandedly applying the law as he sees it—any party coming before the judge taking a position contrary to the judge's view would lose. Second, although "impartiality" in the sense of a lack of preconception in favor of or against a particular legal view may well be an interest served by the announce clause, pursuing this objective is not a compelling state interest, since it is virtually impossible, and hardly desirable, to find a judge who does not have preconceptions about the law. In fact, the state's constitution positively forbids the selection to courts of judges who are impartial in the sense of having no views

Continued on next page.

on the law because all judges must be learned in the law. Third, the Court need not decide whether achieving "impartiality" (or its appearance) in the sense of openmindedness is a compelling state interest because, as a means of pursuing this interest, the announce clause is so woefully underinclusive that the Court does not believe it was adopted for that purpose. This is demonstrated by the fact that statements made in an election campaign are an infinitesimal portion of the statements judges and judges-to-be make that commit them to a legal position, because they have committed themselves before coming to the bench or while on the bench. Such commitments have been made in prior rulings or in nonadjudicatory settings, such as in classes they conduct, books, and speeches. Thus, a candidate for judicial office may make such a commitment before he announces his candidacy or after he is elected. Justice Stevens' asserts in his dissent that statements made in an election campaign pose a special threat to openmindedness because the candidate, when elected judge, will have a particular reluctance to contradict them. While this may be true with regard to campaign promises, promises are not at issue here because they are regulated separately. Also, with regard to nonpromissory commitments to a certain position, it is not self-evident that judges will find these more binding on them than a carefully considered holding. The state (D) has not carried the burden imposed by strict scrutiny of establishing that statements made during an election campaign are uniquely destructive of openmindedness. Justice Stevens is wrong in his broad assertion that to the extent statements on legal issues seek to enhance a candidate's popularity they evidence a lack of fitness for office. Such statements are made in all confirmation hearings, and thus Justice Stevens must think the entire federal bench is unfit. Moreover, the notion that the special context of electioneering justifies an abridgment of the right to speak out on disputed issues sets First Amendment jurisprudence on its head. We have never allowed the government to prohibit candidates from communicating relevant information to voters during an election, but Justice Ginsburg would do so. She contends that the announce clause must be constitutional because due process would be denied if an elected judge sat in a case involving an issue on which he had previously announced his view. She reaches this conclusion because, she says, such a judge would have a "direct, personal, substantial, and pecuniary interest" in ruling consistently with his previously announced view, in order to reduce the risk that he will be "voted off the bench and thereby lose his salary and emoluments," but elected judges—regardless of whether they have announced any views beforehand—always face the pressure of an electorate who might disagree with their rulings and therefore vote them off the bench. If it violates due process for a judge to sit in a case in which ruling one way rather than another increases his prospects for reelection, then by Justice Ginsburg's logic, the practice of electing judges is itself a violation of due process. Finally, although a universal and long-established tradition of prohibiting certain conduct creates a strong presumption that the prohibition is

constitutional, the practice of prohibiting speech by judicial candidates is neither ancient nor universal. The Court knows of no such prohibitions throughout the 19th and the first quarter of the 20th century, and they are still not universally adopted. This does not compare well with the traditions deemed worthy of attention. There is an obvious tension between the state's constitution, which requires judicial elections, and the announce clause, which places most subjects of interest to the voters off limits. The First Amendment does not permit the state (D) to leave the principle of elections in place while preventing candidates from discussing what the elections are about. Reversed and remanded.

CONCURRENCE: (O'Connor, J.) The very practice of electing judges undermines the state's interest in an impartial judiciary. If judges are subject to regular elections they are likely to feel that they have at least some personal stake in the outcome of every publicized case. Even if judges were able to suppress their awareness of the potential electoral consequences of their decisions and refrain from acting on it, the public's confidence in the judiciary could be undermined simply by the possibility that judges would be unable to do so. Moreover, contested elections generally entail campaigning, which can require substantial funds. Even if judges were able to refrain from favoring donors, the mere possibility that judges' decisions may be motivated by the desire to repay campaign contributors is likely to undermine the public's confidence in the judiciary.

CONCURRENCE: (Kennedy, J.) Content-based speech restrictions that do not fall within any traditional exception should be invalidated without inquiry into narrow tailoring or compelling government interests. The speech at issue here does not come within any of the exceptions to the First Amendment recognized by the Court. The state (D) may not censor what the people hear as they undertake to decide for themselves which candidate is most likely to be an exemplary judicial officer. Deciding the relevance of candidate speech is the right of the voters, not the state. Accordingly, the announce clause contradicts the principle that unabridged speech is the cornerstone of political freedom.

DISSENT: (Stevens, J.) The Court's disposition rests on two seriously flawed premises: 1) an inaccurate appraisal of the importance of judicial independence and impartiality, and 2) an assumption that judicial candidates should have the same freedom to express themselves on matters of current public importance as do all other elected officials. There is a critical difference between the work of the judge and the work of other public officials. In a democracy, issues of policy are properly decided by majority vote, and it is the business of legislators and executives to be popular. By contrast, in litigation, issues of law or fact should not be determined by popular vote, and judges

Continued on next page.

must be indifferent to unpopularity. Any judge who faces reelection, however, may believe that he retains his office only so long as his decisions are popular. Nevertheless, the elected judge, like the lifetime appointee, does not serve a constituency while holding that office. Instead, the judge has a duty to uphold the law and to follow the dictates of the Constitution, as well as to make judgment on the merits—not as a mandate from the voters.

DISSENT: (Ginsburg, J.) Elections for political offices, in which the First Amendment holds full sway, must be distinguished from elections designed to select those whose office it is to administer justice without respect to persons. The state's (D) choice to elect its judges does not preclude the state (D) from installing an election process geared to the judicial office. As agents of the people, legislative and executive officials serve in representative capacities, and therefore, candidates for these representative offices must be left free to inform the electorate of their positions on specific issues. Judges, however, are not representatives of particular persons, communities, or parties; they serve no faction or constituency. They must strive to do what is legally right, even in the face of unpopularity. In addition, the majority ignores a crucial limiting construction placed on the announce clause by the courts below. The provision does not bar a candidate from generally stating views on legal questions; it only prevents her from publicly making known how she would decide disputed issues. That limitation places beyond the scope of the announce clause a wide range of comments that may be highly informative to voters, including statements of historical fact; qualified statements; and statements framed at a sufficient level of generality. The announce clause is thus narrower, and campaigns conducted under that provision more robust, than the majority's construction of the clause acknowledges. Judicial candidates may not only convey general information about themselves, but they may describe their conception of the role of a judge and their views on a wide range of subjects of interest to the voters. Further, they may discuss, criticize, or defend past decisions of interest to voters. What they may not do is remove themselves from the constraints characteristic of the judicial office and declare how they would decide an issue, without regard to the particular context in which it is presented. Properly construed, the announce clause prohibits only a discrete subcategory of the statements the majority's misinterpretation encompasses. Moreover, the majority ignores the significance of the announce clause to the state's (D) judicial election system, and its interdependence with the state's (D) rule prohibiting candidates from making pledges or promises of conduct in office other than the faithful and impartial performance of the duties of the office. The pledge or promise rule promotes the public faith in the judiciary by attempting to eliminate the perception that a judge's ruling is merely a quid pro quo for being elected on a campaign promise. The state's (D) interest in the pledges or promises clause is thus significant, and its constitutionality supported. The announce clause is equally important to

achieving these constitutional ends, since, without it, the pledges or promises clause would be weak. That is because without the announce clause, the pledges and promises clause can be easily circumvented by a candidate who does not promise anything, but merely announces his or her position on a given issue. Both the promise and the statement contemplate a quid pro quo between the candidate and the voters, and, contrary to the majority's belief, the nonpromissory statement does nothing to avert the dangers inherent in the promissory statement. The announce clause prevents this circumvention of the pledges or promises clause, and, therefore is an indispensable—and constitutional—part of the state's (D) effort to maintain a healthy judiciary.

▶ *ANALYSIS*

This decision presents the difficult issue of whether the restrictions on certain statements made by candidates for judicial office are impermissible content-based restrictions, or permissible content-based restrictions that survive strict scrutiny based on the government's strong interest in preserving judicial independence and impartiality (and the appearance thereof). Hence, the majority focuses on the content of the speech being regulated, whereas the dissent focuses on the government interest. In 2007, the ABA changed its Code of Judicial Conduct to satisfy the decision in this case by eliminating the announce clause and providing an expanded pledges or promises clause.

■━■

Quicknotes

CERTIORARI A discretionary writ issued by a superior court to an inferior court in order to review the lower court's decisions; the Supreme Court's writ ordering such review.

FIRST AMENDMENT Prohibits Congress from enacting any law respecting an establishment of religion, prohibiting the free exercise of religion, abridging freedom of speech or the press, the right of peaceful assembly and the right to petition for a redress of grievances.

INJUNCTION A court order requiring a person to do, or prohibiting that person from doing, a specific act.

STARE DECISIS Doctrine whereby courts follow legal precedent unless there is good cause for departure.

■━■

CHAPTER 16

Marketing Legal Services

Quick Reference Rules of Law

Ohralik v. Ohio State Bar Assn.

Attorney (D) v. Ohio state bar (P)

436 U.S. 447 (1978).

NATURE OF CASE: Review of order suspending attorney from practice.

FACT SUMMARY: Ohralik (D) solicited two young women who had been in a car accident, visiting one while she was in traction in the hospital.

🏛 RULE OF LAW
A state may constitutionally discipline a lawyer for soliciting clients in person, for pecuniary gain, under circumstances likely to pose dangers that the state has a right to prevent.

FACTS: Attorney Ohralik (D), upon learning about an auto accident involving an eighteen-year-old woman, twice visited her in the hospital, whereupon she orally agreed to allow him to represent her. She later sought to renege on the agreement. He also solicited as a client the woman's passenger. The Ohio State Bar (P) instituted disciplinary proceedings, alleging that Ohralik (D) had violated disciplinary rules barring in-person solicitation of clients. Ohralik (D) was indefinitely suspended. The Supreme Court granted review.

ISSUE: May a state constitutionally discipline a lawyer for soliciting clients in person?

HOLDING AND DECISION: (Powell, J.) Yes. A state may constitutionally discipline a lawyer for soliciting clients in person, for pecuniary gain, under circumstances likely to pose dangers that the state has a right to prevent. A state has a strong interest in preventing the perceived harms of attorney solicitation, these being assertion of fraudulent claims, debasement of the legal profession, and potential harm to the client by overreaching, overcharging, underrepresentaiton, and misrepresentation. The potential for coercion of the prospective client is particularly strong in a face-to-face solicitation, as the attorney, who is trained in persuasion, holds a great advantage over the client, who is at best unfamiliar with the law and may be in a particularly vulnerable situation due to whatever misfortune it was that led the attorney to seek him out. For these reasons, a prophylactic rule prohibiting solicitation serves sufficient state interests so as to pass First Amendment scrutiny. Affirmed.

▌ ANALYSIS

At one time, states imposed a near categorical ban on much of the businesslike aspects of law, such as advertising and solicitation. Many of these prohibitions have been lifted after the Supreme Court began applying the First Amendment to attorney advertising. Solicitation is the one area that has not changed in this regard.

■■■■■

Quicknotes

COMMERCIAL SPEECH Any speech that proposes a commercial transaction, or promotes products or services.

PROHIBITION AGAINST IN-PERSON SOLICITATION The ethical limits placed on attorneys when seeking to enter into a client relationship, preventing attorney from engaging in coercive or improper behavior when contacting potential clients directly.

■■■■■

Zauderer v. Office of Disciplinary Counsel

Attorney (D) v. Ohio state bar (P)

471 U.S. 626 (1985).

NATURE OF CASE: Review of attorney disciplinary proceeding.

FACT SUMMARY: Attorney Zauderer (D) placed an advertisement targeting as clients women who had used the Dalkon Shield Intrauterine Device.

RULE OF LAW
A state may not prohibit legal service advertisements targeting a particular segment of the public.

FACTS: Attorney Zauderer (D) placed in a newspaper an advertisement identifying the "Dalkon Shield" (IUD) and inviting women who had used the device to contact his office about their legal rights. The ad informed the reader that the device had been found to cause various physical problems and that Zauderer's (D) office was handling a number of cases involving the Shield. The state Office of Disciplinary Counsel (P) filed a disciplinary action against Zauderer (D), contending that he had violated state rules against solicitation. The state supreme court upheld the Office's (P) imposition of discipline, and the U.S. Supreme Court granted review.

ISSUE: May a state prohibit legal service advertisements targeting a particular segment of the public?

HOLDING AND DECISION: (White, J.) No. A state may not prohibit legal service advertisements targeting a particular segment of the public. This Court has held that government has an interest in prohibiting advertisement that is false, deceptive or misleading, or that concerns unlawful activities. However, when these interests are not implicated, the First Amendment protects commercial speech. Here, the Ohio State Bar (P) contended that the target advertisement ran afoul of antisolicitation rules. However, it is not clear how the advertisement in question violated these rules. There is no allegation that the ad is false or misleading; in fact, it is not disputed that it is quite accurate. An advertisement such as that at issue here carries none of the potentialities for coercion, overreaching, or intimidation that led this Court to approve of categorical bans on solicitation. Also, there is no evidence that it will "stir up litigation." It is not stirring up litigation to notify people that they may have rights. In essence, there is no substantial governmental interest that is advanced by a blanket ban on advertisements of this type, so such a ban is unconstitutional. Reversed.

ANALYSIS

Legal advertising is commercial speech. Commercial speech enjoys a more limited protection under the First Amendment than most other types of speech. In most situations, the government must show a "compelling" interest to restrict speech. In commercial speech, the government must show a less burdensome "substantial" interest. Even under this standard, most cases involving attorney advertising in the last two decades have gone against the government.

■═■

Quicknotes

COMMERCIAL SPEECH Any speech that proposes a commercial transaction, or promotes products or services.

■═■

Professional Responsibility

Shapero v. Kentucky Bar Assn.

Kentucky attorney (P) v. State bar (D)

486 U.S. 466 (1988).

NATURE OF CASE: Review of order upholding the state bar disciplinary rule.

FACT SUMMARY: The Kentucky Bar Association (D) promulgated a disciplinary rule prohibiting the mailing of advertisements for particular legal services.

🏛 RULE OF LAW
A state may not prohibit the mailing of advertisements to a target audience believed to be in need of particular legal services.

FACTS: Shapero (P), a Kentucky attorney, applied to the Attorneys Advertising Commission of the Kentucky State Bar (D) for approval of an advertisement he wished to circulate. The advertisement would be sent to those individuals who, according to public records, were facing imminent foreclosure. The ad apprised the recipients that avenues for forestalling foreclosure existed and recommended that the addressee call Shapero's (P) office for a free consultation about their rights in this matter. While not finding the advertisement false or misleading, the Commission (D) found it to conflict with Kentucky Supreme Court Rule 3.135(5)(b)(i), which forbade direct mailing concerning a specific legal matter to one believed to require assistance as to that matter. The State Bar Ethics Committee, on appeal, agreed that the rule precluded the advertisement Shapero (P) wished to make but urged the Supreme Court of Kentucky to amend the rule. It modified the rule, but not so much as to legitimize Shapero's (P) letter. Shapero (P) brought an action seeking to have the rule declared unconstitutional. The U.S. Court of Appeals upheld the rule, and the Supreme Court granted certiorari.

ISSUE: May a state prohibit the mailing of advertisements to a target audience believed to be in need of particular legal services?

HOLDING AND DECISION: (Brennan, J.) No. A state may not prohibit the mailing of advertisements to a target audience believed to be in need of particular legal services. This Court has previously held that the First Amendment protects from state prohibition advertising which is neither false nor misleading. On the other hand, the Court has sanctioned the proscription of in-person solicitation. The factors which led this Court to conclude that solicitation could be banned were primarily the inherently coercive nature of in-person solicitation and the lack of tangible evidence, after the fact, of whether the soliciting attorney in fact overreached during the solicitation. While a direct-mail advertisement is to some extent more coercive than a general, nontargeted advertisement, the recipient in

no way can be placed under the same sort of pressures that he could be in a face-to-face situation. Further, unlike in the solicitation situation, the letter itself serves as evidence of whether the advertisement is false or misleading. Since the policy reasons for prohibiting face-to-face solicitation are not present here, the speech in question is protected under the First Amendment. Reversed.

CONCURRENCE: (White, J.) Any discussion as to whether the advertisement was in fact false or misleading is a matter for state court determination.

DISSENT: (O'Connor, J.) The decision today is consistent with the earlier *Zauderer v. Ohio*, 471 U.S. 626 (1985), but that case was decided upon erroneous grounds. That case improperly applied the usual test that commercial speech is constitutionally protected if it concerns lawful activity and is neither false or misleading. With respect to advertisements by regulated professions, the states should be free to regulate if the possibility of misleading advertisements exists. The type of advertisements at issue here certainly contain such possibility.

▶ *ANALYSIS*

A general rule of thumb can be gleaned from the Court's triumvirate of decisions, *Zauderer, Ohralik v. Ohio State Bar*, 436 U.S. 447 (1978), and the present action. It would seem that outright solicitation, face-to-face, can be categorically banned. An advertisement, even one to a target audience and containing illustrations, may be permitted. However, it must not be misleading and must disclose all or most information necessary for a would-be client to make up his mind about using the lawyer's services.

■■■■

Quicknotes

COMMERCIAL SPEECH Any speech that proposes a commercial transaction, or promotes products or services.

OVERBREADTH DOCTRINE (Former Rule 7-3 of the Model Rules) Mail solicitation that targets persons known to need legal services is prohibited if a significant motive for the lawyer's doing so is the lawyer's pecuniary gain.

■■■■

In re Primus

n/a

436 U.S. 412 (1978).

NATURE OF CASE: Review of attorney reprimand.

FACT SUMMARY: The South Carolina Bar reprimanded Primus for forwarding a letter to an individual advising her of certain rights and of the opportunity to receive free legal services.

🏛 RULE OF LAW
A state may not prohibit attorneys from mailing letters to potential clients advising them of their legal rights and of the opportunity to receive free legal services.

FACTS: Primus, an attorney, in conjunction with the American Civil Liberties Union, forwarded a letter to one Williams, who had been sterilized as part of a state regulatory practice conditioning entitlement to welfare payments on sterilization. The letter advised Williams that she had a potential claim against the doctor who performed the procedure, and that the ACLU had a legal staff that could perform free legal services for her. Williams declined to pursue the matter, but the State Bar, under a disciplinary rule prohibiting solicitation by letter, published a letter of reprimand against Primus. The South Carolina Supreme Court affirmed the reprimand, and the U.S. Supreme Court granted review.

ISSUE: May a state prohibit attorneys from mailing letters to potential clients advising them of their legal rights and of the opportunity to receive free legal services?

HOLDING AND DECISION: (Powell, J.) No. A state may not prohibit attorneys from mailing letters to potential clients advising them of their legal rights and of the opportunity to receive free legal services. When legal services are performed as part of an attempt to further a political agenda, such activities constitute a form of expression protected under the First and Fourteenth Amendments. State abridgements on such activities must be narrowly tailored to serve a compelling interest. Here, there can be little question but that Primus' solicitation was part of an effort to advance a political program; the ACLU is well known for taking political positions, and the fact that it might benefit at some later date because of a regulated lawsuit does not alter this. Consequently, Primus' letter was a form of protected expression. The proffered state interest is the prevention of overreaching and intimidation of potential clients. While a state has a compelling interest in prohibiting this behavior, it has not been shown that a blanket prohibition on solicitation by mail is necessary to achieve this end. Since the state prohibition is not narrowly drawn, it is unconstitutional. Reversed.

DISSENT: (Rehnquist, J.) A constitutional inquiry must focus on the conduct involved, not on the possible motives of the participants.

▶ ANALYSIS

This case was decided the same day as *Ohralik v. Ohio State Bar Assn.*, 436 U.S. 447 (1978). These two cases appear to show the outer limits of a state's ability to prohibit attorney solicitation. It would seem that the cases can be read to permit a state to prohibit completely all attorney in-person solicitation. All other solicitations, if politically motivated, must be reviewed on a case-by-case basis.

■=■

Quicknotes

COMMERCIAL SPEECH Any speech that proposes a commercial transaction, or promotes products or services.

FREEDOM OF ASSOCIATION The right to peaceably assemble.

■=■

Glossary

Common Latin Words and Phrases Encountered in the Law

A FORTIORI: Because one fact exists or has been proven, therefore a second fact that is related to the first fact must also exist.

A PRIORI: From the cause to the effect. A term of logic used to denote that when one generally accepted truth is shown to be a cause, another particular effect must necessarily follow.

AB INITIO: From the beginning; a condition which has existed throughout, as in a marriage which was void ab initio.

ACTUS REUS: The wrongful act; in criminal law, such action sufficient to trigger criminal liability.

AD VALOREM: According to value; an ad valorem tax is imposed upon an item located within the taxing jurisdiction calculated by the value of such item.

AMICUS CURIAE: Friend of the court. Its most common usage takes the form of an amicus curiae brief, filed by a person who is not a party to an action but is nonetheless allowed to offer an argument supporting his legal interests.

ARGUENDO: In arguing. A statement, possibly hypothetical, made for the purpose of argument, is one made arguendo.

BILL QUIA TIMET: A bill to quiet title (establish ownership) to real property.

BONA FIDE: True, honest, or genuine. May refer to a person's legal position based on good faith or lacking notice of fraud (such as a bona fide purchaser for value) or to the authenticity of a particular document (such as a bona fide last will and testament).

CAUSA MORTIS: With approaching death in mind. A gift causa mortis is a gift given by a party who feels certain that death is imminent.

CAVEAT EMPTOR: Let the buyer beware. This maxim is reflected in the rule of law that a buyer purchases at his own risk because it is his responsibility to examine, judge, test, and otherwise inspect what he is buying.

CERTIORARI: A writ of review. Petitions for review of a case by the United States Supreme Court are most often done by means of a writ of certiorari.

CONTRA: On the other hand. Opposite. Contrary to.

CORAM NOBIS: Before us; writs of error directed to the court that originally rendered the judgment.

CORAM VOBIS: Before you; writs of error directed by an appellate court to a lower court to correct a factual error.

CORPUS DELICTI: The body of the crime; the requisite elements of a crime amounting to objective proof that a crime has been committed.

CUM TESTAMENTO ANNEXO, ADMINISTRATOR (ADMINISTRATOR C.T.A.): With will annexed; an administrator c.t.a. settles an estate pursuant to a will in which he is not appointed.

DE BONIS NON, ADMINISTRATOR (ADMINISTRATOR D.B.N.): Of goods not administered; an administrator d.b.n. settles a partially settled estate.

DE FACTO: In fact; in reality; actually. Existing in fact but not officially approved or engendered.

DE JURE: By right; lawful. Describes a condition that is legitimate "as a matter of law," in contrast to the term "de facto," which connotes something existing in fact but not legally sanctioned or authorized. For example, de facto segregation refers to segregation brought about by housing patterns, etc., whereas de jure segregation refers to segregation created by law.

DE MINIMIS: Of minimal importance; insignificant; a trifle; not worth bothering about.

DE NOVO: Anew; a second time; afresh. A trial de novo is a new trial held at the appellate level as if the case originated there and the trial at a lower level had not taken place.

DICTA: Generally used as an abbreviated form of obiter dicta, a term describing those portions of a judicial opinion incidental or not necessary to resolution of the specific question before the court. Such nonessential statements and remarks are not considered to be binding precedent.

DUCES TECUM: Refers to a particular type of writ or subpoena requesting a party or organization to produce certain documents in their possession.

EN BANC: Full bench. Where a court sits with all justices present rather than the usual quorum.

EX PARTE: For one side or one party only. An ex parte proceeding is one undertaken for the benefit of only one party, without notice to, or an appearance by, an adverse party.

EX POST FACTO: After the fact. An ex post facto law is a law that retroactively changes the consequences of a prior act.

EX REL.: Abbreviated form of the term ex relatione, meaning upon relation or information. When the state brings an action in which it has no interest against an individual at the instigation of one who has a private interest in the matter.

FORUM NON CONVENIENS: Inconvenient forum. Although a court may have jurisdiction over the case, the action should be tried in a more conveniently located court, one to which parties and witnesses may more easily travel, for example.

GUARDIAN AD LITEM: A guardian of an infant as to litigation, appointed to represent the infant and pursue his/her rights.

HABEAS CORPUS: You have the body. The modern writ of habeas corpus is a writ directing that a person (body) being detained (such as a prisoner) be brought before the court so that the legality of his detention can be judicially ascertained.

IN CAMERA: In private, in chambers. When a hearing is held before a judge in his chambers or when all spectators are excluded from the courtroom.

IN FORMA PAUPERIS: In the manner of a pauper. A party who proceeds in forma pauperis because of his poverty is one who is allowed to bring suit without liability for costs.

INFRA: Below, under. A word referring the reader to a later part of a book. (The opposite of supra.)

IN LOCO PARENTIS: In the place of a parent.

IN PARI DELICTO: Equally wrong; a court of equity will not grant requested relief to an applicant who is in pari delicto, or as much at fault in the transactions giving rise to the controversy as is the opponent of the applicant.

IN PARI MATERIA: On like subject matter or upon the same matter. Statutes relating to the same person or things are said to be in pari materia. It is a general rule of statutory construction that such statutes should be construed together, i.e., looked at as if they together constituted one law.

IN PERSONAM: Against the person. Jurisdiction over the person of an individual.

IN RE: In the matter of. Used to designate a proceeding involving an estate or other property.

IN REM: A term that signifies an action against the res, or thing. An action in rem is basically one that is taken directly against property, as distinguished from an action in personam, i.e., against the person.

INTER ALIA: Among other things. Used to show that the whole of a statement, pleading, list, statute, etc., has not been set forth in its entirety.

INTER PARTES: Between the parties. May refer to contracts, conveyances or other transactions having legal significance.

INTER VIVOS: Between the living. An inter vivos gift is a gift made by a living grantor, as distinguished from bequests contained in a will, which pass upon the death of the testator.

IPSO FACTO: By the mere fact itself.

JUS: Law or the entire body of law.

LEX LOCI: The law of the place; the notion that the rights of parties to a legal proceeding are governed by the law of the place where those rights arose.

MALUM IN SE: Evil or wrong in and of itself; inherently wrong. This term describes an act that is wrong by its very nature, as opposed to one which would not be wrong but for the fact that there is a specific legal prohibition against it (malum prohibitum).

MALUM PROHIBITUM: Wrong because prohibited, but not inherently evil. Used to describe something that is wrong because it is expressly forbidden by law but that is not in and of itself evil, e.g., speeding.

MANDAMUS: We command. A writ directing an official to take a certain action.

MENS REA: A guilty mind; a criminal intent. A term used to signify the mental state that accompanies a crime or other prohibited act. Some crimes require only a general mens rea (general intent to do the prohibited act), but others, like assault with intent to murder, require the existence of a specific mens rea.

MODUS OPERANDI: Method of operating; generally refers to the manner or style of a criminal in committing crimes, admissible in appropriate cases as evidence of the identity of a defendant.

NEXUS: A connection to.

NISI PRIUS: A court of first impression. A nisi prius court is one where issues of fact are tried before a judge or jury.

N.O.V. (NON OBSTANTE VEREDICTO): Notwithstanding the verdict. A judgment n.o.v. is a judgment given in favor of one party despite the fact that a verdict was returned in favor of the other party, the justification being that the verdict either had no reasonable support in fact or was contrary to law.

NUNC PRO TUNC: Now for then. This phrase refers to actions that may be taken and will then have full retroactive effect.

PENDENTE LITE: Pending the suit; pending litigation underway.

PER CAPITA: By head; beneficiaries of an estate, if they take in equal shares, take per capita.

PER CURIAM: By the court; signifies an opinion ostensibly written "by the whole court" and with no identified author.

PER SE: By itself, in itself; inherently.

PER STIRPES: By representation. Used primarily in the law of wills to describe the method of distribution where a person, generally because of death, is unable to take that which is left to him by the will of another, and therefore his heirs divide such property between them rather than take under the will individually.

PRIMA FACIE: On its face, at first sight. A prima facie case is one that is sufficient on its face, meaning that the evidence supporting it is adequate to establish the case until contradicted or overcome by other evidence.

PRO TANTO: For so much; as far as it goes. Often used in eminent domain cases when a property owner receives partial payment for his land without prejudice to his right to bring suit for the full amount he claims his land to be worth.

QUANTUM MERUIT: As much as he deserves. Refers to recovery based on the doctrine of unjust enrichment in those cases in which a party has rendered valuable services or furnished materials that were accepted and enjoyed by another under circumstances that would reasonably notify the recipient that the rendering party expected to be paid. In essence, the law implies a contract to pay the reasonable value of the services or materials furnished.

QUASI: Almost like; as if; nearly. This term is essentially used to signify that one subject or thing is almost analogous to another but that material differences between them do exist. For example, a quasi-criminal proceeding is one that is not strictly criminal but shares enough of the same characteristics to require some of the same safeguards (e.g., procedural due process must be followed in a parole hearing).

QUID PRO QUO: Something for something. In contract law, the consideration, something of value, passed between the parties to render the contract binding.

RES GESTAE: Things done; in evidence law, this principle justifies the admission of a statement that would otherwise be hearsay when it is made so closely to the event in question as to be said to be a part of it, or with such spontaneity as not to have the possibility of falsehood.

RES IPSA LOQUITUR: The thing speaks for itself. This doctrine gives rise to a rebuttable presumption of negligence when the instrumentality causing the injury was within the exclusive control of the defendant, and the injury was one that does not normally occur unless a person has been negligent.

RES JUDICATA: A matter adjudged. Doctrine which provides that once a court of competent jurisdiction has rendered a final judgment or decree on the merits, that judgment or decree is conclusive upon the parties to the case and prevents them from engaging in any other litigation on the points and issues determined therein.

RESPONDEAT SUPERIOR: Let the master reply. This doctrine holds the master liable for the wrongful acts of his servant (or the principal for his agent) in those cases in which the servant (or agent) was acting within the scope of his authority at the time of the injury.

STARE DECISIS: To stand by or adhere to that which has been decided. The common law doctrine of stare decisis attempts to give security and certainty to the law by following the policy that once a principle of law as applicable to a certain set of facts has been set forth in a decision, it forms a precedent which will subsequently be followed, even though a different decision might be made were it the first time the question had arisen. Of course, stare decisis is not an inviolable principle and is departed from in instances where there is good cause (e.g., considerations of public policy led the Supreme Court to disregard prior decisions sanctioning segregation).

SUPRA: Above. A word referring a reader to an earlier part of a book.

ULTRA VIRES: Beyond the power. This phrase is most commonly used to refer to actions taken by a corporation that are beyond the power or legal authority of the corporation.

Addendum of French Derivatives

IN PAIS: Not pursuant to legal proceedings.

CHATTEL: Tangible personal property.

CY PRES: Doctrine permitting courts to apply trust funds to purposes not expressed in the trust but necessary to carry out the settlor's intent.

PER AUTRE VIE: For another's life; during another's life. In property law, an estate may be granted that will terminate upon the death of someone other than the grantee.

PROFIT A PRENDRE: A license to remove minerals or other produce from land.

VOIR DIRE: Process of questioning jurors as to their predispositions about the case or parties to a proceeding in order to identify those jurors displaying bias or prejudice.

Casenote Legal Briefs